Praise for *I Don't Just Work Here*

"A must-read for anyone who wants to create a workplace where employees can thrive. Felicia and Elena provide a clear road map of the big and small actions that we can all take to achieve a healthier workplace culture, no matter who we are or where we work."

—Ashley V. Whillans, PhD,
Associate Professor, Harvard Business School

"People now rate 'My Employer' as the most trusted institution in the world, well ahead of Business and a stunning 60 points above Government in trust. The workplace is also seen as the one place where employees can safely discuss societal issues. This book reinforces that today's employees are values-driven, preferring to work for those employers willing to speak up on the issues of the day. That is why there is indeed a new purpose for workplace culture."

—Richard Edelman, CEO, Edelman

"I have studied forgiveness for more than forty years, leading global research with people on every continent except Antarctica. In *I Don't Just Work Here*, Felicia and Elena illuminate forgiveness and other skills in new, intriguing, and useful ways that will make organizations better if they follow this excellent advice."

—Everett Worthington, PhD, Licensed Clinical Psychologist
and Professor Emeritus, Virginia Commonwealth University

"*I Don't Just Work Here* is like a laser pointer. Elena and Felicia have highlighted a few of the precise things leaders and managers can say and do to set standards and lead their organizational culture forward. The stories they tell stick, and the strategies they offer help people make progress in their lives."

—Craig Wortmann, CEO, Sales Engine, and Founder and
Academic Director, Kellogg Sales Institute, Northwestern University

I Don't Just Work Here

I Don't Just Work Here

The New Purpose of Workplace Culture

Felicia Joy and Elena Grotto

Matt Holt Books
An Imprint of BenBella Books, Inc.
Dallas, TX

Matt Holt is an imprint of BenBella Books, Inc.
10440 N. Central Expressway
Suite 800
Dallas, TX 75231
benbellabooks.com
Send feedback to feedback@benbellabooks.com

BenBella and *Matt Holt* are federally registered trademarks.

Printed in the United States of America
10 9 8 7 6 5 4 3 2 1

Library of Congress Control Number: 2023030571
ISBN 9781637744680 (hardcover)
ISBN 9781637744697 (electronic)

Editing by Katie Dickman
Copyediting by Lydia Choi
Proofreading by Marissa Wold Uhrina and Lisa Story
Indexing by WordCo Indexing Services, Inc.
Text design and composition by PerfecType, Nashville, TN
Cover design by Brigid Pearson
Printed by Lake Book Manufacturing

Special discounts for bulk sales are available. Please contact bulkorders@benbellabooks.com.

This book is dedicated to all leaders who are doing their best to create cultures where excellence is the standard, strong business results are the norm, and people know they matter at work. Building incredible cultures is hard—we think it will always be hard—but it's endlessly interesting and deeply important.

An important note about breaking news as you read our book:

One of the most challenging aspects of designing, managing, and measuring culture in today's business and social climate is the number of contemporary issues that affect our lives and the rapid pace at which the details of those issues—and the best ways of handling them—change. As of the writing of this book, we have included the best available research, proven strategies, and top practices for shaping workplace cultures that inspire employees and drive business results while being responsive to many new expectations. We recognize, for instance, that since we wrote the core content of this book, the Supreme Court of the United States overturned the use of affirmative action as one factor in academic admissions; and since then, some state attorney generals have written to corporations advising that they will pursue legal action if they think the organization's diversity, equity, and inclusion policies and practices are unfair. This backlash against so-called woke capitalism has had a chilling effect on some of the work companies had been doing to address societal issues and injustices. That's just one update on one issue. There are others. There is no way to know what will happen day-to-day but the underlying thinking we have shared in these pages is timeless. Onward!

Contents

PART IV
Learning from Leaders in Action

Introduction

The Chicago River snakes through the downtown area of Chicago, Illinois, with tall, imposing buildings lining both sides. Many boat companies run tours up and down the river, and if you are walking around the surrounding streets, you can see a tour guide standing at the helm of each boat with a microphone in hand, reciting the history of these architectural gems.

In the summer, the tour guides rattle off their script under the warming Chicago sunshine; by fall they may be wrapped in a blanket to guard against the crisp wind or donning a poncho for the occasional rainstorm. They skip winter, and by late spring the guides are bundled in puffy coats, ready for Chicago's signature snow pop-ups as summer once again draws near. The tour guides recite the dates and names of the architects responsible for each building's design, they succinctly summarize the impact of the Chicago Fire on the downtown area, and maybe they crack a joke here and there—the script is similar, day after day; rain, snow, or shine; tour after tour.

Of all the guide companies, the Chicago Architecture Center takes a distinct approach to its Chicago River boat tours. Its corps of specialized guides are all empowered to create a tour script with a unique theme. Sure, they run through all the routine information of a building—an architect's name and tenure at their respective firm—but each tour is strikingly different from the last. One tour might be led by a specialist who works in the fashion industry and therefore speaks about the façades of each building as if describing garments. They might compare the geometric base of Goettsch Partners' 150 North Riverside Plaza to a bold and angular neckline on an evening gown; they might speak about the shiny windows on William Pedersen's 333 West Wacker as if about an elegant sequined skirt; and they might talk about how the dark, vertical lines on the Willis Tower evoke suspenders on a tuxedo.

Another tour might be led by a retired building engineer who explains the feats of plumbing, mechanics, and electricity that ensure the safety and longevity of these mighty skyscrapers—pointing out trapdoors and infrastructure details that you could otherwise miss. The fashion-industry guide sees a building as a tuxedo; the building-engineer guide highlights its masterful snow-removal features. The same building generates remarkably different viewpoints. Members of the public can attend hundreds of Chicago Architecture Center boat tours and hear hundreds of different thematic takes on the buildings lining the Chicago River—each tour rooted in fact but distinct because of the lived experience and unique perspective of the guide.

The Chicago Architecture Center boat tour is an analogy that helps frame how we've developed this book as a result of our unique perspectives. We are business-school professors and advisors to Fortune 500 companies, so our lived experience and unique perspective include working in both academic and corporate settings. Our points of view are also informed by our multifaceted identities, our experiences before and beyond our current work, and—like so many workers—by what we have encountered during the challenges and changes throughout the world since the onset of the COVID-19 pandemic.

Felicia worked in politics, family and children services, marketing, entrepreneurial business ventures, external affairs, and crisis communications before resigning from her corporate job and going back to school full-time to earn her master's degree in behavioral science from Harvard. She's a young Black woman who was born and raised mostly in the American South in Atlanta, Georgia. She also spent a couple of her childhood years in Zweibrücken, Germany, where her mother, who served twenty-seven years in the US Army, was stationed.

Elena came to corporate America by way of the nonprofit industry, working for a decade in a museum and studying art before eventually earning a master's degree in business administration at the University of Chicago Booth School of Business. She's a young white woman, born and raised in a Chicago suburb in the American Midwest with a stint of her childhood spent in Paris.

We met at Edelman, a global communications consulting firm, where our professional interests overlapped and we started working on client assignments in corporate affairs and business transformation together.

With Felicia's background in behavioral science and Elena's interest in the people side of business, we developed a strong portfolio of clients who sought Edelman's guidance on how to define and embed their unique workplace culture so employees would feel a sense of purpose at work and the companies they work for could successfully boost performance and lead in the marketplace.

The business world has evolved markedly in the years since the two of us met and formed a professional partnership. Organizations have navigated everything from the COVID-19 pandemic to the national reckoning after George Floyd was murdered, reputational damage due to cultural incompetence or employee uprisings, supply-chain disruptions, surges in demand met by constrained supply and labor, the pressures of inflation, more frequent environmental disasters, the impact of political division, war, the reversal of *Roe v. Wade*, and more.

From a news-consumption perspective, companies continue to consider what trusted news sources they will use to share their story—toggling between mainstream media's established storytellers and the "real talk" (and sometimes misinformed) voices on social media that can spread stories quickly. And, when it comes to social issues, companies have increasingly veered away from the now-outdated guidance to only address issues that have a direct tie to their business (for example, a consumer packaged goods company commenting on recycling) and have instead stepped into conversations on issues that matter to their people, regardless of business connection—like a consumer packaged goods company commenting on the Supreme Court's decision to overturn *Roe v. Wade*.

These events and changes have resulted in this triggering trifecta that has created new expectations of organizations: (1) a preference for purpose, (2) concerns about boundaries and mental health, and (3) an increasing desire to see businesses lead social change.

Managing people in this climate requires intentionality and hard work, and we would argue that it is a specialized skill—it requires leaders to expertly navigate topics and decisions that are often evolving in real time, conjuring up a range of emotions, and for which there isn't a "right" answer but there certainly can be a "wrong" answer. And the fallout from a wrong move can be significant: calls for leaders to resign, employee walkouts, customer boycotts . . . we've all seen these events on the front page of newspapers and news sites. So what does it take to lead well now? To date, the necessary skills aren't widely taught in traditional business education or in on-the-job training, but, interestingly, our research found that the skills required to bring people together are often taught informally or in programs or development tracks for community or faith-based leaders. That's why we wrote this book. Our perspective is that as business leaders, we can learn a lot from community leaders who inspire and manage in dynamic and sometimes contentious climates like the one we now face.

Regardless of your specific professional responsibilities, it is our firm belief that to rise to meet the demands of the day, you will need to understand the impetus for this significant shift in employee expectations and acquire the mindset and skill set to lead effectively in business. The subsequent chapters outline these changes in far greater detail and delve into the societal forces behind such seismic shifts. This is how we unpack our thesis:

In part one, "A Changed Workplace," we'll introduce a few dominant characteristics of employees today and summarize what these employees expect of their employer, which in many cases is drastically different from employee expectations in previous years. In this section, we've also included a chapter on why this new expectation of workplace culture matters, with a focused review of what's at stake.

In part two, "Managers as Workplace Community Leaders," we outline what it looks like when managers expand their skill set to effectively navigate the new expectations of workplace culture.

Consider this section as a view of what success looks like. As part of that, we have a chapter specifically devoted to a role-by-role breakdown of how to define and manage culture at work. So, for example, if you are in the finance unit or on the Chief Financial Officer track, you can see a snapshot of what your typical responsibility may entail in regard to managing workplace culture and how it overlaps and is distinct from someone in marketing or on the Chief Marketing Officer track. We end this section with a chapter that goes beyond role-by-role implications and speaks to the personal impact of doing this work well.

Following that, in part three, "Workplace Culture Skills," we get into the nitty-gritty. If part two shows you the endgame, then this section is how you get there. It's important that something as expansive as "culture" feels tangible and that you know where to start building it. Each chapter in this section details one of seven skills—and related frameworks—so you know what you need to do and when to enact these skills as you manage and lead your team. Why these seven skills? Based on our research and experience in corporate and academic work settings, it is our conclusion that these are the essential capabilities that people need to navigate the new expectations of employees today. Some are more obvious than others: take, for example, the skill of having a good conversation, which may feel routine to many. As is the case for many routine things in life, we sometimes gloss over the actual mechanics of how to do it, and by studying such, we can drastically improve. Other skills we examine may be surprising, such as forgiveness, which is outlined in chapter twelve. The importance of the ability to forgive was mentioned again and again in our research by professionals of all ages, races, sexual orientations, personality styles, and genders. It appears that our working world is clamoring for clear information on how to forgive. Concrete tips on how to adopt these seven skills is the precise content of this section of the book, and the content includes stories to illustrate key points, overviews of how to live each skill, "notes from the field" on how to avoid pitfalls, and a few top takeaways so you can quickly remember key concepts. We promise this book will read like a field guide, and this section particularly meets that description.

Finally, in part four, "Learning from Leaders in Action," we share vignettes of several professionals who are either masters at doing this work or are candid about how they are trying to learn these skills. These portraits include "real talk" anecdotes that are vivid and relatable, and we suspect they may be some of the lasting takeaways of your experience reading this book. They underscore the contemporary nature of this work—after all, people are learning how to do this right now. You can join them.

Across these four sections, it is an important caveat that, like the Chicago Architecture Center specialists who extensively study the facts of the buildings to create their unique tours, the two of us have merged data with our lived and professional experience in writing this book. Our thesis—that the purpose of workplace culture has evolved from creating an environment that only focuses on building a better product to *creating an environment where people are supported in becoming their better selves*—is rooted in research and direct experience.

However, we are two professionals and academics among millions, and we have all experienced fascinating changes in the working world and will continue to do so. We point this out at the beginning of the book to clarify that while some readers may have workplace experiences that differ from those we discuss, we have spent our professional and academic careers studying people at work, and the following pages are our informed analysis of what has happened as workplace culture evolves and why a keen understanding of this shift matters so much to the success of people and business today and long into the future.

Who We're Speaking to in This Book

This book is primarily for managers and rising leaders who want to boost the success of their teams and organizations by truly understanding and harnessing the power of workplace culture in the contemporary business climate.

While we'll speak to managers and rising leaders most of the time, we will also turn our attention to the C-Suite because the impact and effectiveness of managers and leaders is often bound or enabled by the amount of support, time, and budgets allocated to managers by senior and executive leaders.

Boards of directors also play an increasingly critical role in workplace culture and can stir change in support of middle managers by asking the right questions and making strategic recommendations to executives. Therefore, we will occasionally speak to governance leaders as well. It will be clear when we are speaking to each audience.

We're in This Together

In the subsequent chapters, we will use the collective "we" in our writing because we are two of the many leaders learning to manage the new expectations of workplace culture. This is our shared pursuit.

PART

I

A Changed
Workplace

1

The Working Human
and the Whole Human

The Reason There's Been a Workplace Evolution

People have an instinctive will to survive. This instinct is reflected in our stories about ourselves and the world, whether an ancient parable like the story of the Tower of Babel or an inspirational Instagram post. Our need to survive manifests in multiple ways, including the desire to be a part of a group where we experience a sense of belonging and safety. This group could be our country, neighborhood, family, or team at work.

Some scientists refer to this belonging-to-survive behavior as an example of the *instinct theory of motivation*, which states that certain actions arise from primal, biological needs rather than experience or education. Belonging makes us feel recognized, important, and included. It also helps us feel safe—we seem to instinctively know that in the face of a threat, being a part of a group makes survival more likely than if we were battling a nemesis alone.

History has shown us this is true in cases of environmental disasters, war, famine, and even deadly global viruses, where by working physically apart—but virtually together—people from many organizations and backgrounds were able to innovate and develop effective vaccines. Belonging has helped humankind survive, evolve, and thrive.

It is no wonder employees now crave the option and opportunity to talk about, listen to, and take action on societal issues at work, whereas in the past this was considered forbidden. Legacy social and systemic norms have allowed racial, ethnic, gender, and class supremacy to become entrenched in every aspect of life. Given the human need to belong to survive, these norms are now being challenged and disrupted. Among broad swaths of the public, there is drive for supremacy of any kind to be dismantled and replaced by equality.

Ironically, acts that have been unfair and created inequality are, in some ways, outgrowths of the human will to survive. Clamoring for power and superiority is a survival tactic driven by the attempt to dominate because of fear. In studying the ecology of human fear, we find that this tendency to build protective layers is a misdirected attempt at "survival optimization."

The more layers we can build between ourselves and risks—which, when distorted, means building more layers between ourselves and others—the greater degree of assurance we *feel* that we'll survive when a threat arises. We behave this way in part due to biochemical prompts from our nervous system.[1] However, feelings are not facts, and thus the human instinct to survive by discriminating against others is misguided and is being challenged today in classrooms, boardrooms, virtual rooms, and communities.

Throughout the past, a couple groups have most benefited from social and systemic norms while other groups have been excluded, some to more extremes than others. The people who have been excluded have formed their own groups and communities where they enjoy a sense of belonging and safety. However, changes in demographics and the modern context—such as a younger, more diverse populace emerging in America and around the world—are leading to a shift where more people say they can see the power and benefits of diversity, equity, and inclusion. This constellation of factors has delivered us to where we are today.

French poet and novelist Victor Hugo, who wrote *Les Misérables*, said, "Nothing else in the world . . . not all the armies . . . is so powerful as an idea whose time has come."[2] Indeed, the time for the idea of equality and equity for all—the dream that Dr. Martin Luther King Jr. spoke of so eloquently—has come. Nobody should ignore it, especially employers.

Gartner's 2020 ReimagineHR Employee Survey found that "supporting employees in their personal lives more effectively enables them to not only have better lives, but also to perform at a higher level."[3] The survey found that employers who engage employees at this level see a 21 percent boost in the number of high performers compared to organizations that ignore this opportunity. Another profound insight from the survey puts a fine point on the new expectations of employers: 74 percent of employees "expect their employer to become more *actively involved* in the cultural debates of the day."[4]

The "Whole Human"

This focus on supporting employees in their professional *and* personal lives means that today's employees are showing up at work as what we've come to term "whole humans." Previously, employees often assumed a compartmentalized persona at work, one we describe as a "working human." Working humans certainly had interests beyond their job but were conditioned to mute those interests when at work. Working humans focused on business success, and managers evaluated them based on metrics like productivity, performance, compensation-to-revenue ratios, and aptitude for professional development and promotion. In this environment, there was often a focused effort to create a workplace culture for these working humans, but the purpose was to provide values and behaviors that employees needed to get things done together. In effect, workplace culture was only about work.

When it comes to whole humans, however, the persona at work mirrors a lot of who they are outside of work, complete with varied interests and outlooks. Whole humans certainly care about the business metrics previously listed, but they also actively and openly expect their employer to help them with their needs as they pertain to three primary categories:

- mental and physical health
- societal and cultural competence
- emotional intelligence and maturity

The new purpose of workplace culture is to provide organizational values and behaviors that create trust, belonging, and community by embracing the whole person—and *all* people, those traditionally excluded as well as those who may feel newly alienated, perhaps because they are part of traditionally high-status groups from which diversity efforts appear to be for someone else. Workplace culture today is about caring for whole people. When people feel seen and sense that they belong, they work harder and longer, take more initiative, and are far more committed to the organization even when they could be more highly compensated at another organization.

Why have so many employees metamorphosed from working humans to whole humans, and why now? We believe people have an increased desire to address the tensions at play in society as America and other nations continue to undergo transformation fraught with tension between those who have been traditionally favored and those who have been traditionally marginalized. People want flexibility to live their lives and freedom to be themselves, and the will to achieve this does not conveniently start at 5:30 PM and end at 8:30 AM just after or before work. Moreover, given the habitual living patterns of people, there are few places besides work where they can face or raise these issues and get support to change themselves or demand change from others. Consider these statistics about the United States:

- Educational attainment has risen over the past fifteen years, but still only four in ten Americans twenty-five years of age or older have completed a four-year degree at college—a place where people's worldviews and perspectives are often expanded and reshaped for the first time.[5]
- Most Americans—nearly seven out of ten—live their adult lives in or near the same cities and towns in which they

grew up,[6] rarely having the opportunity to meaningfully interact with people who have vastly different life experiences from their own.

- America has become more diverse, with people of color comprising 40 percent of the population, and this is expected to increase to more than 50 percent by 2044;[7] however, wealth remains higher for white households,[8] and family income, wealth, race, and ethnicity can be strong predictors of opportunities and life outcomes.[9]

- More people are aware of and care about societal issues than in previous years, with 59 percent of Americans saying it is no longer acceptable for companies to be quiet on social-justice matters and 49 percent saying they assume a company doesn't care about social issues if leaders don't speak out on them—both upward-swinging trends.[10]

- Finally, millennials are the largest living generation by population size and at 35% are the largest generation in the workplace by proportion.[11] Fueled by the era of tech-enabled transparency, millennials appear to believe, along with Gen Z, that life is always on, and they have embraced the idea of being more of themselves at work.

Globally, personal and societal changes are translating into new workplace culture expectations as well. A 2023 Qualtrics study with thirty thousand employees in twenty-eight industries across twenty-seven countries (including the United Kingdom, Canada, Japan, Australia, France, Germany, Thailand, Singapore, South Africa, and Colombia) found that "being employed isn't just about having a job—it [has become] a core part of a person's value system" whereby employees who believe that their employers represent their values are 27 percent more likely to have higher engagement scores, 23 percent more likely to work with their current employer for three or more years, and 20 percent more likely to have higher well-being scores.[12]

In a 2022 Bain study with ten thousand employees in seven countries (the United States, Canada, Australia, the United Kingdom, France, Germany, and Italy), researchers found that across attributes including race, ethnicity, gender, sexual orientation, geography, function, industry, and level in the organization, people defined inclusion similarly but rarely felt it: *70 percent of employees do not feel fully included.*[13]

It is at this intersection of the new expectations of business and the strains of change in America and around the world that an increasing number of employees are showing up at work not just for a paycheck but also for an opportunity to grow as people and as part of a group that is pursuing something bigger than itself.

But why are we turning to our jobs to find a sense of community and serve as a hub for collective social purpose and whole-human personal development? First, it's important to recognize that even with an enduring focus on "work–life balance," now more contemporarily referred to as "quiet quitting," people still use a lot of their daily time for work. The average person now spends at least one third of their life at work—even if being "at work" means attending Zoom meetings from the corner of your (bedroom) office or kitchen table. That alone is a significant statistic, but once you consider that another third is spent sleeping and the final third is spliced across family responsibilities, housework, shopping, personal care, cooking and eating, socializing with friends, education, leisure, exercise, television, reading, and more, it becomes clear that for many, our time at work is a substantial and sometimes the most dominant part of our entire life.

As mentioned, in the United States it was once a workplace cultural norm to "check your feelings at the door." Sure, we made social bonds with one another, spoke openly about our children or family, chatted about holiday plans and vacations, and cheered for our favorite sports teams. However, no matter how close colleagues grew, there was a conscious expectation to avoid political, social, or cultural issues that could stir emotions or division in the office.

This can be traced back to the Protestant work ethic that has been cited in social science as a cornerstone of capitalism and the value system that defined the rise of the industrial age and American work life. This perspective over time has resulted in strong signals from the top, with CEOs traditionally avoiding discussion of potentially controversial topics and preferring to focus their remarks exclusively on earnings reports, product launches, geographic expansions, organizational changes, or significant leadership transitions. They spoke about business, period.

It was as if companies existed thirty thousand feet above the hot-button news of the day. Those CEOs who did comment on divisive contemporary issues could see their stock price dip and, in some cases, were taken to task by their boards.

However, the COVID-19 pandemic shifted the purpose of work for many people. Though it seems long past, we raise this pivotal and historical time because it was an irreversible turning point in how people view work and the value of their time while on the job. Gartner released results of a survey that described how, while "82%

of employees say it's important for their organization to see them as a person, not just an employee, only 45% of employees believe their organization actually sees them this way."[14] Purposeful work, which perhaps was a "nice to have" for many people pre-pandemic, seems to have become a primary focus for many people. The Gartner researchers refer to this as "The Great Reflection" and explain that many people "have developed a new sense of self-awareness and worth" as they consider the role of work in their lives, the effort they want to put in, and the value they want to receive. McKinsey cites research finding that 91 percent of US employees now expect employers to care about their emotional health.[15]

Therefore, whole humans not only have new expectations of employers; we also have new expectations of ourselves, and we increasingly show up to work online or in person with the intention to discover, debate, digest, and act on the most pressing issues of our time—even if the issues are not directly related to the core business of the organization where we work.

Employees are not alone. Consumer and investor expectations of the workplace have changed, too: 68 percent of adults say CEOs should step in and act when government fails to fix societal problems,[16] and 61 percent of institutional investors say they have increased their asset allocation to companies that excel on environmental, social, and governance factors.[17] Holistically, these expectations have created a new mandate for business and a new purpose for workplace culture: Go beyond only focusing on a better business or customer experience to more intensely focusing on a better employee experience. Support and help employees to lead better lives. Manage for whole humans, not just working humans.

The Benefits and Challenges of Managing Whole Humans at Work

As managers, we may feel more comfortable having tough conversations with working humans about performance issues, sales targets, hiring strategies, and more. These situations require business acumen. The abilities to develop and demonstrate cultural competence, have tough conversations about mental and physical health, and act with emotional intelligence and maturity require growth and a unique skill set. While "people skills" are certainly helpful for managing working humans, many managers in businesses have been successful without them. By comparison, managing whole humans *requires* advanced-level people savvy, substantial self-awareness and personal growth, and an astute understanding of contemporary news and culture.

Bill George—a senior fellow at Harvard Business School and former chairman and CEO of Medtronic, a $108 billion–dollar global Fortune 500 company—said, "Over the years, there has been a massive change in leadership expectations. The baby boomers followed a chain-of-command leadership style influenced by World War II. Those days it was all about maximizing shareholder value. Moreover, jobs were limited in the '60s, and securing financial independence and the necessities of life was the priority. Fast forward to today, and millennials and Gen Z are passionate about working for a purpose. They want a workplace that offers diversity and inclusion, supports climate plans, and makes the world better for everyone."[18]

Managers and leaders may resist these new expectations, questioning why they were hired to run a P&L but are now expected to, say, check in regularly on someone's mental health or emotional needs in response to news reports on a recent racial incident or ruling by the Supreme Court. The oft-repeated line "It's not personal; it's just business" has seemingly been replaced with "It's personal *and* it's business."

Despite some resistance, the new expectations of workplace culture are here to stay. We caution that this can be challenging for those who see these shifts and wish the workplace would "go back to how it used to be" when things were "far less complicated" and the job focused solely on managing working humans, not whole humans. Perhaps work felt less complicated to certain populations back then, but this mindset doesn't adequately consider how complicated the workplace may have always felt to people who are part of historically disenfranchised communities. Those who have had to quietly squash their feelings on racism, sexism, homophobia, ageism, political discrimination, or any given issue non grata have had to manage complicated feelings only in "safe spaces" or closed-door gatherings facilitated by employee resource groups devoted to discussing and celebrating specific communities or topics—or simply never at work.

Coinciding with these expectations is the increased realization of the need to meet them because of employees' role in an organization's success. A 2021 Edelman Trust Barometer special report found that, for the first time, employees had become the most important stakeholder to an organization's long-term success—outpacing customers, clients, and shareholders. While the rankings fluctuate, for as long as these data points have been collected, employees remain number one or two on the list—a sea change from the days when only customers were king. The importance of employees, combined with their new perceptions of work and life in general, has created a population that knows its value and power with employers. What are employees doing with this newfound confidence? Workers are often looking for a company that talks about and takes action on issues that align with their values. In the 2022 Edelman Trust Barometer, six out of ten employees say they choose their employer based on beliefs, and the same percentage of global employees expect their employers to take a stand on societal issues that they care about.[19] Further, these employees want employers to use their resources to be a purposeful part of addressing some of the world's toughest issues, such as climate change and decarbonization, systemic racism, human trafficking, LGBTQIA2S+ rights, and gender and pay equity.

When employers can create a sense of belonging based on shared values, which subsequently attracts and retains top talent, the benefits to the bottom line are significant. A 2019 article in *Harvard Business Review* noted that "high belonging was linked to a whopping 56 percent increase in job performance [and] a 50 percent drop in turnover risk," among other returns. The researchers went on to quantify the implications, noting that a sample ten thousand–employee company could see savings of approximately $52 million over twelve months.[20] But perhaps equally stunning about this research was the authors' explanation that a lack of belonging—a sense of exclusion (which we have found can in some cases come from misaligned values)—can cause the same sensation as physical pain. In an era when so many workplaces are focused on wellness, the notion that employees might feel pain if the culture does not evolve to meet these new expectations is a clear and preventable risk.

If employees are certain about what they expect and there's a financial rationale for employers to evolve the workplace culture to account for these expanded needs, why is it so hard to deliver on these new expectations? It goes back to the fact that this isn't just about intent. Sure, some companies *want* to do better, but as the aforementioned Harvard researchers note in straightforward lay terms, "companies are blowing it." Let's get on to how to solve that.

2

What's at Stake:
Silence Speaks Volumes

Despite all the data and anecdotal evidence that the world has changed and employees not only expect but also need an evolved approach to workplace culture, we have seen resistance by some CEOs and other influential executive and senior leaders who prefer the status quo. They would like to keep workplace culture in the mode of yesteryear, when it was for the working human, not the whole human, and when it was concerned only with productivity, not also purpose.

Business history is littered with examples of companies and leaders who slipped away to irrelevance, or eventual failure, because they simply could not accept that change was afoot and that they needed to adapt regardless of their personal opinions or tastes. These failures to change have related to business models and strategy as well as culture. This includes Blockbuster being sidelined by Netflix; Motorola and Blackberry losing to the Apple iPhone; Borders being overcome by Amazon; and Kodak being overtaken by the digital cameras of Canon, Nikon, and smartphone makers.

Kodak is among the most interesting of these companies because it was at one point way ahead of everyone else, having produced digital photography technology in the 1970s, a full thirty years before it became popular enough among consumers to take off. Its resistance to change, however, allowed competitors to catch up, leaving the lagging Eastman Kodak company to file for bankruptcy.[1]

Today Kodak sells products and services for commercial printing and packaging and trades on the New York Stock Exchange for less than $5 per share. It is not completely out of business, but it is a shadow of the company it once was after having grown over the course of 130 years from its founding in 1888. In the past, it was the top untouchable leader in the photography category with a vertically integrated brand. In 1975, Steven Sasson, a twenty-four-year-old engineer who had just begun working for the company a couple years prior, invented the digital camera. He showed the technology to the management and marketing executives of the company, but they were focused on their dominance of the photography film market and doubted anyone would ever want to look at photos on digital screens.

Sasson's digital-camera invention from the '70s is now on display at the Smithsonian National Museum of American History in Washington, DC. In 2009, he was recognized in a ceremony at the

White House by US President Barack Obama, who awarded him the National Medal of Technology and Innovation.[2] Sasson will forever be lauded for his ingenuity. Kodak may forever be remembered for its failure to change.

The negative effects of a resistance to change are not limited to instances of market demand and business strategy; there are direct risks of resisting employee feedback about workplace culture. In the mid-1990s, management at a global tire and rubber company decided to increase work shifts from eight hours to twelve hours and decrease new hire pay by 30 percent. Employees expressed their dissatisfaction with the decision and, as organized labor, sought to negotiate with leadership to revert to the hours and pay they felt they deserved. Discussions reached gridlock, and the workers went on strike. The company responded by hiring replacement workers. Plant employees went on strike or working without a contract for about three years, and more than one thousand replacement workers took on their jobs. Millions of tires were produced and distributed to the marketplace during this time.

In the fall of 2000, the company announced a recall of 6.5 million tires because of a tread-separation safety defect that put drivers at risk of dangerous and, in some cases, deadly blowouts. The tires were recalled in numerous countries, including the United States, Venezuela, Ecuador, Thailand, Malaysia, Colombia, and Saudi Arabia.[3] In the weeks following the recall, the company's stock-market value tanked 55 percent from $16.7 billion to $7.5 billion, revenues sharply declined by 30 percent, and the corporation ultimately reported a loss of $750 million for the year. Additionally, the company eventually had to pay a settlement of $240 million to one of its top car-manufacturing customers, when the National Highway Traffic Safety Administration found the company at fault for the safety defect.[4]

Years later, two economists at Princeton analyzed data that would have typically been proprietary and restricted but had become publicly available due to litigation and congressional investigations. They were evaluating the relationship between employee experience (or "labor relations") and product quality, asking the question: Do workers provide more effort and due diligence if they feel they are treated better?[5] Through statistical methods and analyses of timing, the economists found correlations between employee dissatisfaction and the defective tires. They were able to rule out the likelihood of other plausible explanations for the product quality defects, including blame that may have been placed on replacement workers, by calculating the distribution of defect claims on a month-by-month basis; the claims reached excess peaks for tires produced when the experienced laborers had returned from strike. Ultimately, they found that "tires that were made in [the plant] during the labor dispute were at least fifteen times more likely to have resulted in a claim than were tires manufactured in other plants."

Today the company has a market cap of nearly $26 billion, more than 135,000 employees worldwide, and comprehensive policies and plans to cultivate a healthy workplace culture. We do not know what it is like inside the company, but its strategies are inspiring and promising with, as an example, its B-Olympic program, which addresses employee well-being. The company says it measures its progress monthly with pulse surveys and aims to elevate psychological well-being, social well-being, physical well-being, and its workplace environment. It has also publicly declared a commitment to adhere to the UN Guiding Principles for Business and Human Rights and the International Labor Organization's Declaration on Fundamental Principles and Rights at Work.[6]

Just as some companies have initially resisted change and only adjusted after massive losses or failed to adapt to change before it was far too late, others have seen changes unfolding and chosen to act decisively, pivoting and evolving to a strategy and business model that can fit the new needs and direction of the world.

In 1925, the boll weevil, a beetle not native to the United States, migrated to America and ruined cotton crops throughout the American South as it fed on cotton buds and flowers. With the regional economy devastated, the government and private-sector corporate leaders came together to conceive a plan to end the insect's devastation ahead of the next crop. Huff-Daland Dusters were launched to provide aerial crop-dusting services to treat the cotton and protect against the beetles. Spraying pesticides from these planes worked well for the intended purpose and was aligned with the norms of the times. Over time and through the Great Depression, the Huff-Daland company evolved, expanding its business to include aerial surveying, mail-carrier services, and eventually passenger services. It even operated internationally in Lima, Peru. Today the company has 83,000 employees and a market capitalization of $20 billion and is one of the top and longest-operating passenger airlines in the world with its main hub at the world's busiest airport (Hartsfield-Jackson Atlanta International Airport). It is now known as Delta Air Lines, the brand name it claimed in 1945.[7] Can you imagine where Delta would be today if it had tried to maintain a crop-dusting business with all the concerns about chemicals, pesticides, bioengineered food supply, and environmental pollution? It would be defunct. But it is not. It is a leading company in its industry because its leaders accepted change and adapted.

These two paths—embracing change or resisting change—and the fates at the end of them await companies, CEOs, boards of directors, and executives as they stand at the crossroads of workplace culture today and make their decisions on which way they will go.

Some executives are resisting change by standing idly and remaining silent, hoping that the new needs of employees and the new expectations of all stakeholders are a trend that will be as short-lived as the latest social-media challenge or news cycle. They want to simply continue with or go back to the way workplace culture always was with few to no changes. But their silence is speaking loudly. Today, silence can be a clear decision in the minds of current and prospective employees as well as observant stakeholders, including investors. There are other CEOs who are resisting change but are doing so proactively with candid narratives on how the new generation will be less well prepared, and less in many other ways, unless it adheres to the workplace culture norms of the past. These CEOs remind us of the executives in the Kodak boardroom presentations when Sasson showed the digital-camera technology he had developed and they thought a critical mass of people would never be interested in digital pictures in the long run because they were so focused on the power and profits they had at the time.

Today, we could liken ourselves to Sasson. CEOs, boards, and executive leaders: the workforce has changed. A growing number of people want to work at companies where purpose is evident in the organization's values, behaviors, and ways of working. They want to be part of workplace cultures where they can bring their whole self, or at least more or most of their self, to work. That means employees don't want to pretend that the most critical and pressing issues of our time, and daily occurrences related to these issues, don't matter to them. They matter very much, and people want to talk about them. The fact that some people on a team might not have the same perspective is not an excuse or reason to forbid these conversations or to relegate them to only employee resource groups. The majority of employees believe you should put forward the budget to enable them to have managers who are properly educated and trained to facilitate these conversations in groups and to converse well with individuals on their teams. They also believe you should be investing in their development, and they want to hear your position on these issues and see you leading on them in the world and giving people opportunities to contribute to societal change as well. Here, in this book, are the insights and the data to make the choice to lead your company in a direction that will position it to remain highly relevant, competitive, profitable, and in the lead.

One Last Word on Resistance to Change

Bob Kegan is a clinical psychologist, adult-development theorist, and professor emeritus at the Harvard University Graduate School of Education. Broadly, Dr. Kegan is known for Constructive Developmental Theory and his insights on adult-behavior change, which he has studied for more than twenty years. He wrote about these in his book *Immunity to Change: How to Overcome It and Unlock the Potential in Yourself and Your Organization.* He is also known for his insights on workplace culture, which he wrote about in *An Everyone Culture: Becoming a Deliberately Developmental Organization.*

Dr. Kegan's theory and ideas on human progress and purpose are profound. In one of his workshops led with his close collaborator, Lisa Lahey, and attended by a writer for *O, The Oprah Magazine*, writer, he discussed why people have such a hard time changing. Dr. Kegan says our resistance to change is a behavior that makes sense once we uncover the anxiety or fear that we are subconsciously protecting ourselves from when we feel deep down inside what the change could mean for us. In the workshop, Dr. Kegan used the example of Patrick, a former workshop participant he describes as a "superstar CEO." Drs. Kegan and Lahey, and Patrick himself, acknowledge that he is the kind of disciplined and thorough person who decides he is going to achieve a goal, follows through, completes it, and is satisfied—so Patrick is perturbed that he has not been successful in "softening his top-down management approach" as he would like. Patrick then fills out several columns on a handout, clearly stating his goal. In the first column, he notes that he wants to be more of a delegator and listen to ideas from his team more often. He then notes in column two that he is getting in his own way by interrupting his team when they talk, not seeking out their ideas proactively as he said he would like to do, and not loosening the reins enough for people to feel they have the actual authority and support to make decisions. These are all ways that Patrick is sabotaging his goal.

This leads to a question Drs. Kegan and Lahey offered in the workshop: What would happen if you stopped the behaviors that are getting in the way of achieving your goal? (For Patrick, this meant all the behaviors we just discussed: interrupting others, not seeking their feedback, and hovering so they do not feel fully empowered to make decisions without him.)

Holly Brubach, the *O* reporter, writes that Drs. Kegan and Lahey went on to say that "this is the moment Patrick the CEO realized that if he did delegate, he would lose the sense of himself as 'the super problem solver, the one who knows best, the one who is in control—yesterday, today, and tomorrow.' Patrick's mind was in the grip of equal and opposite impulses, prompting him to describe himself as having 'one foot on the gas and one foot on the brake.'"[8]

Could it be that the CEOs who are silent (but therefore loud) or actively resisting changes to workplace culture that are counter to their personal preferences are stuck, like Patrick, between accommodating employees' needs and preferences and remaining comfortable by leaning into their own desires? If you are a CEO or executive and have any doubts as to whether you are having the Patrick problem, we invite you to step away from your own perspective and opinion, even if just temporarily.

Write down all the strengths of your preferred approach to culture, then write down the possible weaknesses. Do the same for the culture that others around you are advocating for or that you sense others want. Consider both workplace culture approaches from the persona of various people who work at your company. You may even take this a step further and actually have a trusted advisor or leader talk to a few different kinds of people at your organization to hear how they feel about the two workplace culture approaches. Take it all in, and remember the fate of companies that hold fast in the face of change. Now, revisit your decision and do what you feel is best.

PART

II

Managers as Workplace Community Leaders

3

How to Manage Whole Humans

New Skills for New Needs

In *The Intern*, Robert DeNiro plays Ben Whittaker, a seventy-year-old retired businessman and widower. To stave off retirement boredom, he applies for an internship at a hot new e-commerce startup. From his interview and through his daily experience after getting the job, the movie is a comedy of small to significant errors in the workplace related to culture and the dynamics between managers and teams and between colleagues.

For instance, during Ben's interview, one of the hiring managers unwittingly asks him where he sees his career in five to ten years. Just a minute too late, they both realize and laugh at the fact that the manager should have considered that the routine interview question wasn't relevant or a good one for Ben, who is of the age where people stop making these kinds of decisions about what should happen in the next few years when they are statistically likely to be deceased.

In another scene, the administrative manager and executive assistant to Anne Hathaway's character, Jules, who is the founder and CEO of the startup, displays dramatic signs of anxiety, burn-out, and escalating mental-health risks. She talks about how hard she works and how much effort her work takes, though she doesn't think Jules notices or cares. She has a loud, public episode that nobody nearby is professionally equipped to handle.

These experiences are funny in the movie because they are comedically played, but in real life they aren't funny at all. They are examples of how and why workplace culture must adapt to the new context, needs, and expectations of the modern workforce and society—across a varied and complex set of employee needs and preferences.

Gallup research shows that 70 percent of employee engagement is localized,[1] meaning engagement is based on the experiences people have every day at the team level. Additionally, Edelman found in its Trust in the Workplace research—with seven thousand respondents from around the world in countries including the United States, the United Kingdom, Brazil, China, India, Germany, and Japan—that 69 percent of workers globally look to their workplace as the second most significant source of community, after family and friends.[2] Distilled to an actionable insight, these findings suggest that managers and the four to five people each of us works with most often every day shape the majority of our sense of culture and community at work. The manager of a team is the key leader within this frame. Thus, it is now a critical imperative to prepare managers to act not just as skilled *business* leaders but also as skilled *community* leaders who create connection, engagement, and a purpose-driven work ethic because they understand and motivate their teams from a place of mutual trust.

Developing a Community Leader–Like Manager

To become a business leader with a community leader–like presence, we as managers have to first make a shift in our thinking, followed by changes in our focus and behavior. During this transformation, it is critical to reject the notion that the new expectations of employees will automatically render today's managers as either naturally good at "this type of thing" or, conversely, fundamentally unable to grasp the new skills needed. Managing whole humans is not an innate skill, and in today's environment it can be quite delicate and complex. Thus, this new managerial mindset relies on seven skills that most managers can learn or sharpen. We have identified these skills through research and direct professional experience working with teams and clients of all sizes:

1. Conversing
2. Listening
3. Empathizing
4. Decision-making
5. Representing others
6. Persuading
7. Forgiving

First, a Shift in Thinking

"I cannot overstate the importance of a leader or manager saying [to an employee], 'I care more about your well-being than I do about your results,'" said Adam Grant, a world-renowned organizational psychologist and researcher, in an interview on organizational resilience.[3]

If you're a business leader, Grant's bold declaration may worry you. Managers of people within profit-making companies are traditionally accustomed to thinking about and leading the working human rather than the whole human. You might wonder whether leading with this well-being-before-results mindset would signal or outright convey to your teams that performance at work isn't as important as their feelings. The natural result if people perceived a well-being-first message as a license to relax and slack off would be your company losing competitive ground. That would be a deal-breaker, and this discussion would be over. But only if that were true. It is not. The data show the exact opposite. There is a direct correlation between the extent to which employees feel trusted to be responsible and do their jobs well and their willingness to extend trust to leaders in the workplace. For example, in an Edelman study, out of the 71 percent of employee respondents who felt their CEOs trusted them, 87 percent trusted their CEO and 90 percent trusted their manager—whereas employees who felt their CEO did not trust them (29 percent) also had low trust, with only 27 percent trusting their CEO and 43 percent trusting their manager.[4]

The people-first mindset will lead most employees to trust you more and work harder for you than they otherwise would because you will have first showed that you trust them and demonstrated that you care about their holistic well-being.

That's good news because the well-being-is-a-priority paradigm is central to managing and leading whole humans in this new societal context where people expect businesses to build *shared* value, not just shareholder value. Leaders who have adopted this mindset care a great deal about both productivity and people, with the care of people taking the lead because those who have tried it know that enhanced productivity will follow. The business results of leading this way speak for themselves.

Then, a Shift in Skills and Behaviors

In addition to adopting a people-first mindset, managing whole humans requires adopting or leaning further into the new or newly emphasized skills we noted:

Conversing

As managers, we need to demonstrate through our conversations that we truly hear and see our teams and are thinking about ways to help them grow. This will equip our teams to display this behavior to one another as well. This is what creates a sense of community and belonging.

Listening

A study by the American Management Association found that 59 percent of respondents do not believe management listens to their concerns.[5] As managers, when we show that we have listened not only by making reference to what our teams have previously shared but also by acting on it, we build a greater sense of trust and connectivity in our team.

Decision-Making

Managers who have good judgment, pursue equitable choices, and make decisions that are clearly in line with the organization's and team's values will find that even when their teams are not in unanimous agreement on a given topic, they remain unified. When managers model strong decision-making, people are better able to disagree and commit to moving forward because their leaders have cultivated an atmosphere of trust and all team decisions stem from a point of integrity and equity.

Representing Others

Many decisions are made with a few leaders bringing perspectives and insights from their teams and business units. Our employees are not always present in key meetings to speak for themselves. They must rely on their managers to represent them and their interests. As managers, when we are able to equitably and powerfully represent every member of our team in a way that creates opportunities, we have a material impact on our employees and the trajectory of their careers. This is a huge driver of retention and builds additional strength in the culture of an organization where people stay and grow because they are being recognized and getting promoted as a result.

Persuading

In adopting a management posture similar to a community leader's style, we must be able to convince our teams to follow us, which is based on actions and proof, not simply words. That means that we must also be able to convince senior and executive leaders to channel resources—such as investments in our team—in a way that helps our people grow the business and develop our teams. This is based on driving performance and being able to articulate a narrative that promotes that performance.

Forgiving

The ability to forgive is perhaps the most surprising new skill we as managers must develop to be effective within corporations as both business leaders and community leaders. Research cited in the Greater Good Science Center magazine from the University of California, Berkeley, underscores forgiveness as an overlooked but important skill in the workplace.[6]

The article says researchers found that "a lack of forgiveness negatively affects the individuals involved and organizations as a whole. Holding on to negative feelings after a conflict may lead to disengagement at work, a lack of collaboration, and aggressive behavior. Carrying a grudge is also associated with increased stress and a host of negative emotions, including anger, hostility, and vengeful rumination." As managers, we need to engender the behavior of forgiving by displaying it ourselves. By showing that forgiveness is an important skill for community, we will see a notable difference in our teams and in our overall organizational culture.

Empathizing

It's critical to note that underpinning each of the prior six skills is the seventh skill—a super skill—empathy, which is foundational to managing workplace culture today. We'll get more into this in chapter eight.

Closing a Significant Gap in Business Education and On-the-Job Training

Traditional business education and on-the-job training include curricula on listening, decision-making, and persuasion, so some leaders already have some experience with a few of the skills for which we advocate, but the full spectrum—and the relationship that each of the skills has with each other—is now a clear gap in management education and on-the-job development. For the most part, these skills are not explicitly taught in business school, especially not within the context of designing inclusive and purposeful workplace cultures and employee experience. Nor have most leaders who received their skills through workplace learning and development been trained in these areas with a specific focus on culture. The good news is some strides are being made.

We are adjunct professors in the strategy section at the University of Chicago Booth School of Business—a top-five business school in America. In 2021, we created one of the first courses solely focused on workplace culture. Of the top ten business schools in America, few have courses on or related to workplace culture. The same is true of the top twenty global business schools. In 2022, however, some of the top schools announced new MBA majors that would enable students to learn more about and specialize in diversity, equity, and inclusion and other areas of focus related to workplace culture and leading business with a focus on society as well.

The Aspen Institute, a global nonprofit organization established in 1949, was created to pursue the mission of "realizing a free, just, and equitable society." As part of its work, it founded a business and society program in 1988 to advocate for the idea that corporate business and investment decisions should be aligned with the long-term health of society and the planet. Perhaps as a testament to how challenging it can be to change the status quo, the Aspen Institute in 2017—after nearly seventy years of operating—created the Ideas Worth Teaching Award to acknowledge professors and business schools that are starting to teach the kinds of courses that address "the role of business in creating a sustainable, inclusive society."[7]

In spring of 2022, Harvard Business School announced the launch of its Institute for the Study of Business in Global Society. The school said that the institute would be a research-based platform to study the role of business in societal issues by

> integrating and amplifying work already underway . . . and catalyzing new streams of inquiry . . . to direct the tools and resources of Harvard Business School directly towards the critical areas where business and society overlap and occasionally collide. Rather than presuming a single purpose for the profit-making firm, the Institute will gather a community of scholars, students, practitioners, and policymakers to

re-examine and explore the appropriate role for business in a complex and challenging global society.[8]

These decisions and new initiatives by the Aspen Institute, Harvard Business School, and other long-serving, highly reputable institutions and organizations demonstrate the realization that this is an extraordinary gap in business education and corporate competence. Over the next several years, as a new wave of business leaders graduate from these new programs, we will see better-prepared and better-performing corporate leaders and organizations. Until then, this gap remains current and urgent.

4

This Is Not the Work of HR Alone

The phrase "That's not my job" can be said in many work-place scenarios. It can be liberating when someone tosses you a terrible task and you sit up straight in your chair and point out that you won't be taking on this new project because it's outside of your job description. Or perhaps you've been presented with a stretch opportunity that isn't part of your day-to-day work, and you've responded with "That's not my job" and ended up regretting saying so. After all, doing work outside of your direct responsibilities can be an effective way to meet new colleagues, develop additional skills, and establish yourself as a go-getter. Or perhaps you've said "That's not my job" as a way of setting appropriate work–life boundaries, or you've resisted saying that because doing a task is just the right thing to do, such as when someone leaves the office feeling ill and you chip in to be sure their work is covered while they're tending to their health. The point is, every employee likely has had an internal dialogue about when to use the "It's not my job" line and when not to—it usually is a judgment call with some nuance involved. Workers would exhaust themselves if they constantly reviewed their job description and compared what they were hired to do and what they actually do.

Job descriptions posted today don't typically state that candidates should have the skills needed to adapt to the new context, needs, and expectations of the modern workforce and society or, more specifically, be prepared to talk about the most important societal issues of our time as part of their day-to-day experience at work. Now, you could argue that no job description posts that a manager is expected to demonstrate common niceties, such as asking how someone's birthday party was or listening to highlights of a recent vacation. However, as noted in previous chapters, the ability to navigate this new purpose of workplace culture takes concrete skills that must be developed over time, so one could argue it should be noted prominently as a requisite capability. But for what jobs? Is this the work of some but not all?

"That's the job of HR" is a common refrain when it comes to tough conversations at work, and that is true. Those in human resources—or, as it's increasingly termed, the "people," "human capital," or "talent" department—must be experts in guiding workplace conversations, but this important culture work is increasingly relevant in jobs running up, down, and across the organizational chart. Finance, check. Operations, check. Customer experience, check. Strategy, check. Digital advertising, check. Individual contributor, check . . . you get the point.

In the *Harvard Business Review* article "HR Can't Change Company Culture by Itself," author Rebecca Newton summarizes the culture-change process as "really only successful and powerful when business leaders see it as *their* responsibility, and see HR as a resource for helping them achieve it."[1]

So, if HR is a *resource* to help a company navigate the new purpose of workplace culture, what is the necessary skill set and mindset that employees in every other function must bring to the table to collectively create and sustain a workplace culture that meets the evolved expectations of today's employees? Also, importantly, when everyone is responsible for something, there's a high risk that no one owns the work. If the project-management adage "A dog with two owners starves" is true, then imagine the calamity if there are hundreds or thousands or tens of thousands of employees owning this culture "dog."

Author Denise Lee Yohn writes in her *Harvard Business Review* article "Culture Is Everyone's Responsibility," "Importantly, this model doesn't relegate culture-building to an amorphous concept that everyone influences but no one leads or is accountable for. Shared responsibility for culture throughout an organization involves different people and functions within the organization playing different roles in developing and maintaining the culture."[2]

In the previous chapters, we outlined that, increasingly, the role of the CEO is to be savvy as the figurehead of managing whole humans, but what exactly should today's finance leaders focus on? What about a middle manager? The remainder of this chapter covers two stories that demonstrate the types of ways in which various roles can advance this shared ownership of a workplace culture. Certainly read the components that best reflect your current role, but also read the others, as it's important to understand the nuances in roles as teams collectively manage this shared charge. And, critically, these stories should equip you with a quick rebuttal if someone says to you, "That's not my job." The reality is that this work is now an important part of everyone's job.

A caveat before we get started—these stories are fictious but explore real issues companies face today. This is how the storytelling will unfold: first, there's a synopsis of the business and the culture scenario at play, followed by a breakdown of the roles that a variety of functional leaders, middle managers, and individual contributors play in managing the issue. We do this twice—the first story is a scenario at an established company, and the other story takes place at a startup. We've chosen these two settings because the maturity of an organization can lead to different approaches in effectively managing workplace culture.

Scenario #1 Overview—An Established Company

A thirty thousand–employee healthcare organization welcomed a new CEO in February 2020, just before the COVID-19 pandemic. By mid-March, the new CEO (let's call him Dave) assumed the role of a "wartime leader" in that he increased his visibility and everything he said tied back to one thing: rallying the workforce to provide outstanding patient care during the pandemic crisis. Well, mission accomplished, because the communities in which the organization operated continued to have access to exceptional care throughout the crisis.

However, like so many organizations that provided essential services during the pandemic, the aftermath of such hard, focused work was that by 2021, employees were showing signs of acute burnout. Subsequently, the organization had record-high turnover of frontline positions (especially nurses) in the months now commonly referred to as the "Great Resignation." At the same time, employees were clamoring for support in talking about their mental-health challenges at work. Whereas they had compartmentalized their angst during the pandemic because of Dave's effective call to action—and the purpose that unified the workforce, "Access to a healthy lifestyle is a human right for all"—now they were clamoring for mental-health support, space to recharge and refocus on their personal lives, and concrete action to create policies that supported their health and wellness.

Specifically, the policies they wanted were all related to having more flexibility to manage their care, personal obligations, *and* responsibilities at work. While the workforce appreciated that their hospitals and outpatient clinics relied on care teams being present to see patients, many employees balked at being present when they were not providing actual care. Specifically, a group of employees who held particular influence (the people you should know to get the real scoop) summarized this as, "Being healthy is more important than being seen at work."

Another challenge dominating this organization's agenda was that as society moved into a new phase of the pandemic, with restrictions lifted for several months and then reversed as new variants surged, the financial performance of the organization was erratic and far off forecast. The executive team was staring down a significant budget shortfall heading into 2022.

Scenario #1 Roles and Responsibilities

Dave the Chief Executive Officer

Summary

- *Mindset:* Adapting our culture to meet the evolved expectations of our employees is a top priority because our people are the linchpin of a successful business.
- *Goal:* Build C-suite-wide consensus around the role of an employee-centric culture in driving business results; frame employee and board remarks through the lens of culture.

Dave knew he had to invest in workplace culture to get the organization out of its financial challenges, but he was wary of three things:

1. He didn't want to add more work to his already strapped workforce.
2. He didn't want anything he did to be labeled as "Dave's thing"—he knew he needed widespread buy-in.
3. Whereas he was ready to sponsor this people-focused work, he wanted a partner who could connect with the workforce; after all, he's a numbers guy who can rally the troops from a podium, but this workforce that demanded "real talk and real action" intimidated him.

Dave started by addressing item #3, and he hired a new Chief People Officer who would be his partner in this work (the previous HR lead was hugely capable in HR compliance issues but agreed that a People Officer was a gap at the organization to deal with a changed workforce). To his surprise, his preferred candidate stated as a condition of accepting the job that she wasn't going to take on the work of "real talk" with employees. Instead, she said, Dave had to own this work. She, however, would sit next to him—on Zoom or in person—at any events, such as employee town halls, conversations, remarks, etc. He could toss her questions that he didn't know how to answer, but he would be visible and talking—constantly. He agreed to this, and she accepted the job.

Regarding item #2, Dave turned to data. He marched into the first C-suite-wide meeting of the year with a slide on the ROI of culture. He said something to the effect of, "These numbers are staggering—if we invest in our people, then we will be investing in our business. This is my top priority to get us back on track financially, and if it's my top priority, then it needs to be each of yours."

Dave moved on to #1 and, working with his CPO and Chief Strategy Officer, instituted four new projects:

- He established a policy that people managers could adopt flexible scheduling when and where possible to mediate some of the burnout.
- He would go to his people instead of them coming to him: Dave blocked off sixty minutes of each Monday to go to a hospital site and walk the halls, join huddle meetings, or sit down with employees at lunchroom tables (his CPO would, of course, be by his side).
- He partnered with a local university's mental-health experts to develop a weekly five-minute employee podcast that had

quick-to-learn and research-backed ideas on how to effectively manage the emotional and physical health of yourself
and others.

- He charged his C-suite with coming up with a program
  unique to each function that would specifically support people managers in developing the skills to talk about mental
  health in their teams; each leader was paired with a partner
  from the university, and together they developed manager
  support materials (tool kits, activation plans, and conversation scenarios). He avoided a centralized model because of
  the unique needs and schedules of each team.

Dave became relentless in his pursuit of these four projects;
they were practically all he talked about. If he was presenting
to the board on the organization's finances, he started by giving
a report about these four programs before pivoting to discuss
financials. When he ran into someone in the elevator, he always
steered the conversation to one of these four programs. When an
employee collapsed at work, he held a town hall the next day to
remind all employees of the programs and took thirty-five minutes
of questions about how progress on the health of employees and
the overall culture was going. And further, when he was featured
in external media, he would talk about his employees and their
health, full stop.

Culture change is slow, and it takes humans multiple times to
hear something before they believe it, but Dave stayed the course,
being relentless about his message and focus—all the while working to dig the organization out of its financial hole.

Jody the Chief Financial Officer

Summary

- *Mindset:* I understand the correlation between culture and our financial outlook.
- *Goal:* View costs associated with strategic culture programming as a sound business investment and frame employee and investor remarks through the lens of culture.

Jody left the C-suite meeting with Dave fired up. She was going to have to prove that these added expenses were going to *help*, not *hurt*, the organization's balance sheet at a time when she was trying to find significant savings to offset the budget shortfall. She sat down at her desk and started scribbling questions in her notebook. The questions mostly focused on all the new expenses she would need to add to the P&L statement. But one thing Dave had said was sticking with her—"If we invest in our people, they will invest in our business." That made her think of the inverse—"If we don't invest in our people, they won't advance our business."

With that in mind, she started working on two pro forma P&L statements: one that would show the costs of these added programs that Dave had announced and another that would show the risks of not proceeding with these culture investments. For the first P&L, Jody reluctantly plugged in the salary costs of a new C-level position for the CPO, then added significant administrative and legal fees to build this new flexible-schedule policy, added some more modest travel dollars to support the CEO visiting so many hospital sites, and, ultimately, put in a notable sum for contracting the university to create the learning partnership.

Next, she pivoted to the "what if we don't invest in our people" P&L scenario. To do this, she asked herself three questions:

- How might revenue be impacted if employees start voicing their discontent with the organization?
- Are there cost-of-goods-sold risks associated with our culture issue? What are examples?
- What expenses would be impacted by our culture issue?

Most of her responses to these questions pointed to one fact: if the organization developed a reputation as a company that didn't respect mental-health challenges, that could affect its credibility in the healthcare industry, which would add further complexity to the financial outlook. One by one, Jody ticked through the P&L line items and noted hypothetical financial impacts:

- *Marketing and advertising:* The organization already aggressively marketed and advertised its work in both community and national outlets, but Jody ticked this number up by an additional $1 million to demonstrate that to support sustained patient volumes, the company would need to surge advertising costs to counteract the effect of a dip in reputation. She also considered that their crisis consultant would likely end up being looped in again to help mitigate public-relations issues, and that always comes with a significant cost.
- *Charitable care:* The organization had always made significant investments in charitable care, but Jody also increased this line item. Her thinking was that the organization would be under laser focus from charitable partners—many of

whom addressed issues pertaining to or related to mental illness—so it would need to more visibly demonstrate the commitment to being a good health partner, addressing the issues of the community more broadly. This was a frustrating expense for Jody to put in, given that they already spent so much in this area, but she reminded herself that optics are important, even if expensive.

- *Employee benefit programs:* Jody then thought about the cumulative stress and shame that would come if the organization developed the external reputation of being lax on—or, at worst, dismissive of—employee mental health, so she increased the employee-benefits line item; her calculations factored in the expense of an ethics and counseling employee hotline and additional benefits offered to employees if the organization needed to up-level its benefits to prove its commitment. *This could really balloon,* Jody began to think.

- *Recruitment and onboarding:* Finally, she thought about attrition. If the public reputation were damaged, both staff and consultants could begin leaving at an alarming rate. This included losing the investment already made to recruit high-profile doctors.

After totaling up the two scenarios, the disparity was significant. The costs of investing in the culture programming that Dave had outlined were minor compared to the financial expense that could be incurred if they did not take cultural action. Jody was equipped with her financial scenario planning; she would check her calculations with partners in HR, operations, marketing, community relations, and the CEO's office before framing the costs as *risk mitigation* in a presentation to the board.

Dee the Chief People Officer

Summary

- *Mindset:* I need to ensure there are people thinking about the big-picture vision of our culture work but also the nuts and bolts of day-to-day implementation; middle managers are critical partners in this work.
- *Skill set:* Build C-level buy-in for culture work and focus on culture as a driver of attraction/retention strategy.

Dee was energized. She had joined this organization because she felt like Dave viewed her as a strategic thought partner, not simply the "HR person." Dave had been clear that she would have a voice in crafting the strategy for the organization's financial turnaround.

She was proud of the programmatic changes that he had announced at the C-suite meeting. She knew that increasing his leadership presence was essential, and flexibility in scheduling was a benefit that could set them apart from peer healthcare organizations. Additionally, she was confident that the smart university partners they had contracted for the mental-health five-minute course content would do exemplary work; she had contracted them in a previous role. What was tripping her up, however, was the challenge of supporting middle managers in this refocus on mental health and workplace culture at large.

Dee knew that it was one thing for Dave to say from a podium, "Bring your whole self to work; we are here to help you live a mentally healthy life," but a whole other issue when a colleague has a panic attack in front of their manager in the hallway. What should that manager actually say and do? Dee knew that managers need specifics and ongoing support.

Dee didn't love that Dave had tasked each function with coming up with its own plan. She worried that could lead to variance in approach and a lot of redundant work. She wanted to coordinate a working group to help advise each function. Sure, functional leaders could customize the work based on their teams' day-to-day responsibilities, but Dee wanted a consistent team to oversee the strategy of these plans.

She knew that her HR colleagues would jump at the opportunity, but she got up from her desk and walked down the hall in a different direction, toward the offices of the Chief Operating Officer. Her thinking? Middle managers don't simply need more toolkits and memos from HR, even though, yes, those resources are critically important. What they need in addition to those is to be supported by the routines and policies that guide how work gets done. After all, if Dave was saying employees should prioritize their mental and physical health but teams were still underwater because of overly taxing administrative protocol, then there would forever be a disconnect between what they were encouraged to do and what was possible. COO Corey was sitting at his desk, and Dee walked right into his office to speak with him.

Corey the Chief Operating Officer

Summary

- *Mindset:* I need to work in lockstep with the CPO so our operations are coupled with clear behavioral expectations.
- *Goal:* Roll out new operations and clarify existing operations with clear behavioral expectations.

Corey was surprised to see Dee. He figured she had been instrumental in Dave's announcement, and now it felt like she had kind of tossed a lot of the work to others to execute; the university was managing the learning courses, Dave was doing the CEO tour, the specifics of the new flexible-work policy were largely settled— so now it really was a communications issue. Why was Dee here to see him, specifically?

Corey was a consummate professional, so he hid his skepticism when Dee implored him that they needed to become fast-working partners. Her argument: the fourth action item that Dave had announced was dependent on a quick but careful audit of their operations. She said that their two teams could do this together, and their work would answer two questions:

1. What operational considerations could stall or stop a manager's proclivity to talk about mental health with their teams? (Dee made the distinction that it's one thing to learn how to host a conversation, but what if there aren't adequate spaces for having these conversations in private? What if managers encounter technological issues when connected with their remote-hybrid teams?)

2. What operational considerations are taking excessive time away from our managers? (Again, Dee made the distinction that if even if a manager knows how to facilitate this new kind of culture in their teams, they still need the *time* to do so. What are the most labor-intensive processes that pull managers away from their people?)

Corey was less interested in item #1 because he saw it as something he could quickly deputize to the facilities team, but he did find #2 a compelling challenge. He had long heard gripes about the organization's overreliance on process. This could be an interesting opportunity to have his team identify the top three processes that were most burdensome to staff and replace them with something new. He agreed with Dee that he could co-lead this work with her. He said he would pull together three people from his team, and he asked her to do the same.

The group was up and running one week later, starting with focus groups in key workforce segments. They were laser focused on finding which operational procedures were taking up the most unnecessary time at work.

Meera the Chief Strategy Officer

Summary

- *Mindset:* I need to view our CPO as a principal partner in executing our strategy.
- *Goal:* Analyze company culture through the lens of "This focus on people is part of our business strategy."

CSO Meera was confused about her role in advancing Dave's priorities. Her priority for the year had been on increasing operating margins. For the past year, she had managed to margin with a focused cost-cutting approach (reduced staffing and service levels, given how the system had shifted away from surgical care and elective procedures during the COVID-19 pandemic). However, now that they were emerging into a new phase of the pandemic, she was tasked with finding new strategic approaches to achieving a strong operating margin. Additionally, the hospital system had two other strategic focus areas: successfully migrating a significant number of surgical procedures to ambulatory facilities, and pursuing and stewarding smart partnerships that would ensure the organization was leading on value-based care, including telehealth and virtual health options. How exactly did these three strategic "pillars" relate to Dave's mandate? She decided to go talk to Jody to get the perspective of a CFO.

Jody walked Meera through her P&L exercise, and Meera found it a compelling way to consider the costs—and potential savings—associated with Dave's culture focus. She decided to do something similar. She mapped out the business strategy as her three initial pillars of operating margin, ambulatory facilities, and partnerships, but she put "a workforce culture focused on health and flexibility" as a foundation below all three. She could continue talking about the same three areas of her business strategy, but she would do so by emphasizing that to ensure each pillar is possible, people need to be healthy and have the flexibility they need. After sketching this out, she set up time to review it with Dave, as he would need to similarly talk about people as the

THIS IS NOT THE WORK OF HR ALONE

foundation to the business strategy in all his board and leadership remarks.

Beth the Chief Marketing Officer

Summary

- *Mindset:* I need to work in lockstep with the Chief People Officer to ensure our brand strategy is aligned to our workplace culture.
- *Goal:* Align customer (or in this case, patient) journey to employee journey and plan for any misalignments.

CMO Beth immediately put time on Dee's calendar and included the Chief Legal Officer in the meeting. Her concern was a recent advertising campaign that her team had just rolled out across the region. The ads were all about mental health, imploring the community to prioritize themselves and come to this healthcare system for the very best care. She wanted to know: What would happen now that Dave was going to parade around the system admitting that their own people were having a mental-health crisis? Were they at risk for legal exposure? Did they need to pull the ad campaign?

Beth and Dee met later that day, and Dee felt a bit blindsided. How had she not heard about this ad campaign before? Why was there such little communication between the marketing team and the people team? Beth didn't seem surprised; after all, they had completely different audiences. Their customers—their patients—had entirely different needs from those of their employees.

That's when Dee cut in. She implored Beth to think about this differently moving forward. Today's customers and employees talk to one another, are one another, and look to each other for information on brands that they want to buy *and* work for. The customer/patient experience and the employee experience must be aligned, or else the company is open to significant vulnerabilities. Beth pointed out that, in essence, she had been thinking that when she suggested this meeting in the first place—she thought that these billboards proclaiming that they were the destination for world-class mental-health care might land very poorly if their own people couldn't get the support they needed at work.

Beth and Dee decided that their two teams had to start talking to each other regularly. And they would facilitate this by assembling a tight team of the following people:

- Talent-acquisition lead
- HR business-partner lead
- Mental-health campaign lead
- Mental-health patient coordinator
- Dee and Beth

These six people would meet the next day in a room with a huge blank wall. Bringing stacks of sticky notes, they would plot out the patient journey for someone in mental-health care *and* the employee journey. Their goal would be to start the long, hard work of understanding where the patient and employee journeys aligned (from a messaging and experience perspective) and where there were major gaps. Dee and Beth agreed that this was going to be a slow project that would likely illuminate more gaps than they could tackle right away, but it was the right place to start.

Andrea the Board Chair

Summary

- *Mindset:* I believe metrics on culture are as important as financial performance in guiding this company forward.
- *Goal:* Outline expectations of which culture metrics should be evaluated for inclusion in quarterly reports.

Andrea, the health system's board chair, received an unplanned call from Dave, which was not entirely out of the ordinary. They had a good rapport, and in addition to their formally scheduled meetings, he gave her a call about once a month to ask for real-time advice.

Andrea could hear a lot of energy in his voice; he shared that he felt he was doing the right thing, even though this was stepping out of his comfort zone. She felt he was right—he was endlessly confident when talking about numbers, so to hear him now talking about his people as the most important asset was a new message. However, it was one she agreed with. It seemed that every day the *Wall Street Journal* published an article that outlined the downfall of a CEO who was promoted for their specialized expertise only to struggle with managing their people.

Andrea listened to Dave's summary and immediately challenged him with one question: How will you know these four programs that you've outlined are working? Dave's response was okay, but a bit weak. He spoke about how his team would be watching two things: attraction and retention metrics, and the annual employee-engagement score.

Andrea responded that those were fine things to watch in the long term, but she thought that Dave could show more frequent updates to the board. She started spouting off other, more real-time metrics that his team could collect:

- Number of calls to ethics hotline
- Exit-interview sentiments
- Employee-satisfaction pulse surveys
- Amount of time to fill open roles
- Percentage increase or decrease in applications
- Initial-offer acceptance rates from prospective employees

Andrea had to run to another meeting, but she asked Dave to continue thinking on this. She suggested that he form a team to develop a culture-issue dashboard. They could watch these metrics and report at the quarterly board meetings. She reminded him that he'd started the call by saying that if he invested in his people, they would invest in the business. So, she said, let's create a dashboard that proves that to be true. Dave ended the call by saying that he would get someone moving on a dashboard to demonstrate short-term progress.

Manager Anjuli

Summary

- *Mindset:* I understand that fostering culture is a top priority at work.
- *Goal:* I know the nuts and bolts of how to build a culture that meets the needs of today's workforce, specifically what to say and do and how to do it, and I also understand the partners that I must engage to execute on these expectations.

Anjuli oversaw catering operations for the organization and reported to COO Corey. She happened to have her monthly 1:1 meeting with Corey the same day as Dave's C-suite meeting about the renewed focus on culture. Anjuli walked into Corey's office and could feel some tension. She asked how he was doing.

Corey opened up that he was frustrated because a series of the new culture priorities had taken him by surprise at the C-suite meeting. Anjuli listened and responded that she had some key points for Corey to raise to Dave, or even to Dee, the CPO:

- Seven years ago, the former CEO, Carol, had gone on and on about this thing called "Culture Week." Carol had announced it at a town hall, and there had been posters and banners, T-shirts, water bottles, etc., advertising the event. The problem, Anjuli explained, was that Culture Week seemed to be about *giving* employees things but not *doing* anything impactful. She even mentioned that she had been miffed that the organization was spending so much money on inconsequential giveaways (such as water bottles) while employees were told they needed to forgo merit raises that year. About two years after Culture Week launched, it disappeared with no explanation. She said she was sharing this story because her team of legacy employees would likely remember this, and it would be important to convince employees that this new focus on culture would be different from the botched Culture Week of yesteryear.
- She also shared that she was happy to hear she would receive training on how to talk about mental-health issues

with her team. She appreciated that the organization was going to invest in her professional development, but she had a request—since several of her team members (specifically those who managed vendor relationships) were remote employees, she would need specific training on leading in a remote environment. She said that she could envision how she would broach tough topics in her in-person team meetings, but it felt awkward to bring these up on a Zoom call. Corey wrote down this consideration.

Corey then asked her if she was already discussing issues of mental health with her team. Anjuli said she'd had one conversation of importance about a month ago. A new colleague of hers had returned to work after a week caring for a sick child. Anjuli had asked this person how she was holding up after such a tense personal time. The employee had responded that she wasn't okay, but she would be eventually. That answer worried Anjuli—she didn't know if it was a subtle call for help. Instead of pressing her colleague on what she meant, however, Anjuli had decided to just state that she took issues of mental and physical health seriously and that the employee assistance program was a strong resource for those who needed support. That was the extent of the conversation. Anjuli asked Corey if he would have handled it any differently, and Corey said he thought she did just fine. He said he'd have to learn himself what additional things he could say or do in that same situation.

Individual Contributor Mariah

Summary

- *Mindset:* I understand why my company is focused on culture; I see the connection between this focus and my work.
- *Goal:* Understand what specific day-to-day actions I need to take to act on company values and behaviors.

Mariah was contacted via the office of the COO to participate in a focus group about processes that run counter to a culture that values mental health. Mariah's to-do list was a mile long, but her manager had suggested she prioritize attending the focus group—after all, Mariah had heard that this project was the CEO's priority, and because she was vying for a promotion, she wanted to demonstrate she was doing work that advanced the business.

She would find time for the focus group, but her bigger concern was what the organization would do about all the signals she was used to receiving about speed and influence being more important than health. For example, just in the past week, Mariah had seen the following:

- An employee being reprimanded for letting an email that was sent at 10:15 PM go unanswered until the next morning
- A manager rolling her eyes when someone on the team shared that they had been struggling with depression and needed help with a deliverable
- A colleague known for setting unrealistic deadlines and delivering disparaging personal insults being promoted to a new role with increased responsibility
- A peer collapsing at work and then, rumor had it, going on mental-health leave

Mariah appreciated that the organization was talking about mental health, but she was skeptical that anyone would do work that would make an impact. She also wondered why the leaders were coming to her, given her junior stature in the company. What could she, as an individual contributor in finance, do? Nothing, she guessed, but the focus group invite said, "We all have a role to play in this work." She wondered if someone was going to explain to her exactly what that meant.

• • •

Scenario #1 and the characters outlined above detail an example of culture work for those who are part of a large, established company. The employees are operating in an organization with routine processes, legacy behaviors, and an established reputation with employees, consumers (in this case, patients), and other key stakeholders. Some implications of this environment include the following:

- There are job descriptions and established routines for each role, so, notably, the culture responsibilities detailed above are likely in addition to their already packed days; these scenarios should give a quick example of how to leverage the skills someone *already has* to accommodate culture work at all levels and disciplines.
- There is a history and legacy reputation to manage. "This is the way we always do things" is such a powerful force in established companies, and when it comes to the new expectations of workplace culture, it is important to signal

that this is a new day with new expectations or to clearly state why the long-held ways of working will continue to support the business strategy of today.

Doing this work in such a setting is markedly different from doing similar work in a startup environment, which also needs to prioritize culture work at all levels and roles of the organization, however small it may be. Scenario #2 and another cast of characters, below, demonstrate what this work can look like when little—if any—infrastructure or history exists. Notably, you'll see an example of how to approach this work during the early days of a company, when the pressure to scale and get investors locked in is the absolute focus—twenty-four hours a day, 365 days a year— with no end in sight for work that is new, relentless, risky, frenetic, thrilling . . . you get the picture.

• • •

Scenario #2 Overview—A Startup

Three former fashion-industry employees were six months into launching a startup focused on an innovative fabric that was made from recycled paper and could be used for high-quality outerwear. The cohort had arranged itself as a C-suite, with CEO Chana, COO Jamie, and CFO Lane. These three had worked together in the ultra-competitive New York fashion world, where the "sink or swim" expectations had motivated each of them to step into stretch roles, sharpen their influence skills, and do anything to get ahead. This had paid off—they were savvy operators, well connected with a deep "Rolodex" of business contacts, and each was confident in her ability to do anything to which she put her mind. So when Jamie had convened the group and pitched her idea for this new company, they had mapped out a nine-month exit plan from their established jobs and made it happen.

The day-to-day operations of this new company ran largely like their corporate fashion gigs had. With three dominant personalities fighting for attention and each trying to outpace each other, it was an intense place to work. The trick was, it didn't feel intimidating to them—they saw themselves as highly competitive, but because they all wanted the same thing, the atmosphere seemed supportive and inspiring. The high stakes and chaos of it all was a motivator to each of them. However, they had been trying to hire a fourth position for three months. They were looking for a junior "generalist" who could work on all facets of the business. They explained the role as someone who could dive into social-media content one day and then focus on the financial books the next.

They kept almost finding candidates, in that someone would interview several times but then withdraw from consideration just before an offer was made. This was proving to be a costly pattern. The team would spend time wooing and interviewing a candidate just to have them express disinterest once they were far along the candidate-consideration funnel.

Chana decided to figure out what was at the root of this pattern, so she asked two of the previous candidates if they would take a ten-minute call with her. What she learned was fascinating—both candidates said that the mission of the company was attractive, but they had found the competitive vibe to be a misfit with their personal style. One went so far as saying that, usually, social-impact businesses are filled with nice, mild-mannered people. Cutthroat people who want to make the world a better place? She found this aspect confusing and, to a certain extent, off-putting.

Chana disagreed with the candidate's conclusion that purpose-driven companies cannot be competitive, but she found the feedback illuminating. She realized that when it came to workplace culture, their startup needed to be explicit about its expectations. By not clearly stating what it was like to work there, they had lost control of the message, and now people were making their own assumptions about their culture instead. And these assumptions were costly to the company.

Chana had an idea for how to find the right person for the company. She brought the following insights to her team:

- There's a misconception that social impact and competition are mutually exclusive. This could be our competitive differentiator for our culture and talent strategy.
- We don't need to change, necessarily, but we do need to codify our unique culture and explain what it's like to work here so our employees know what's expected of them.
- Competition and unethical behavior can get lumped together if there isn't a clear definition of each. Let's define what our position is so we can use it in recruiting and hiring.

Scenario #2 Roles and Responsibilities

Chana the Chief Executive Officer

Summary
- *Mindset:* I need to assemble a team that has the skills to clarify what we stand for.

- *Goal:* Define a position on social impact and frame employee and investor remarks through the lens of culture.

Chana decided to run a three-hour workshop with the rest of the team to gain clarity on who they wanted to be as a company and how to articulate it to outsiders, including future hires. She blocked off a slot on the team's calendars and started planning the work. After taking a few days to brainstorm how she would run this meeting, the agenda unfolded as follows.

9–9:20 | The Business Problem

Chana opened the meeting by quantifying the money lost during the recent search for their generalist. She did this by calculating the number of hours the entire team had spent recruiting, interviewing, and so on. Then she summarized the two conversations she'd had with the former candidates and put up a slide that read, "Competition and Social Impact Can Coexist," and used that assertion to focus the team for the day. She announced that, by noon, this team would create one purpose statement, three core company values, and three key behaviors. Then they would all be equipped to better talk about the expectations of this generalist role and find people who were strong cultural fits.

9:20–10:20 | The Purpose Statement

Chana set a timer for sixty minutes and led a session on the company's purpose. She started by putting a slide up on the screen that read, "If this is what we do—*Repurpose the world's paper into beautiful, sustainable outerwear*—then <u>why</u> do we do it?" She expected her partners to lose interest in this quickly, so she used a conversational trick she often used with her kids—ask "Why?" five times, which eventually makes for very good conversation. This is how it went:

Chana: Why do we do what we do?

Jamie: Because we were sick of our previous jobs.

Chana: Why?

Jamie: Because each year felt the same—same routine, same people, same pressures.

Chana: Why?

Jamie: Because I never felt like we were making an impact on anything—we were just repeating ourselves.

Chana: Why?

Jamie: Because there are real problems out there, and I want to work on them with the same focus and quality that I brought to my previous work.

Chana: Why?

Jamie: Because I believe things can be beautiful and good for the world at the same time.

Chana: Now we're on to something. Could we claim to be about aligning seemingly opposing forces?

Lane: Yeah, it's like we're about beauty and being good for the world; we're high fashion but sustainable. Is there something there?

The group then had a robust discussion about whether their purpose was about their product or about proving that apparent opposites are not so opposite after all. Chana kept an eye on the timer and summarized the conversation when they had about ten minutes left. She advocated that their purpose statement be "To protect bodies from the effects of climate change without contributing to climate change." The group liked this a lot for three reasons:

1. It was specific enough—it alluded to their product being outerwear without making their purpose solely about clothing.
2. It connected their work to a larger societal good.
3. It was written in a tone that was on brand for them.

10:20–11:20 | Values

Next, Chana led a session on values with the prompt of "If our purpose is 'To protect bodies from the effects of climate change without contributing to climate change,' then what are our beliefs?"

They wrote down ideas on about fifty Post-its, and Chana grouped them into themes. Ultimately, they came up with three values:

1. We believe in technical perfection.
2. We believe that a small group of people can make a true impact.
3. We believe that we don't have time to waste.

11:20–11:50 | Behaviors

Finally, Chana led a session on their ideal and expected behaviors or actions. She did this by using the values and asking:

1. If we believe in technical perfection, then how do our people need to act? The answer they came up with: "We measure twice and cut once."
2. If we believe that a small group of people can make a true impact, then how do our people need to act? The answer

they came up with: "We are minimalists—in our processes with our spending and with ourselves."

3. If we believe that we don't have time to waste, then how do our people need to act? The answer they came up with: "We move fast and don't dwell on failures or feelings."

11:50–12:00 | Culture Summary

Chana ended the day by summarizing their newly formed culture:

Purpose: To protect bodies from the effects of climate change without contributing to climate change.

Values:
We believe in technical perfection.
We believe that a small group of people can make a true impact.
We believe that we don't have time to waste.

Behaviors:
We measure twice and cut once.
We are minimalists—in our processes with our spending and with ourselves.
We move fast and don't dwell on failures or feelings.

Jamie the Chief Operating Officer

Summary

- *Mindset:* I need to translate our culture into operational details and expectations.
- *Goal:* Roll out new operations and clarify existing operations with clear behavioral expectations.

COO Jamie left the workshop with an internal list of things to do. Because their company wasn't large enough yet to have an HR leader, she was playing that role and was therefore the person driving the hiring process for this generalist role. It had become a thorn in her side, specifically because she had assumed it would be filled quickly—*How hard can it be to find someone who wants to work with former leads in the fashion industry?* she'd thought. Turns out, it was much harder than she'd anticipated. But with their newly articulated purpose, values, and behaviors, she thought she could be more explicit about not just what this person would do but also the kind of culture in which they would work. She liked the idea about emphasizing that this was a place where people moved quickly. Maybe by being clear they would attract people who liked that kind of work environment. She revisited her online posting for the role and updated it with the new cultural messaging.

Two weeks later, Jamie had a new candidate in the pipeline. She had done an initial screen and liked that the candidate, Leon, was a competitive, no-nonsense type. Leon had asked Jamie a question, however, that Jamie didn't have the answer to. Leon had said he was surprised that their culture explicitly said they didn't "dwell on feelings." He'd wondered what that meant. For example, did they talk about their lives outside of work? Leon had mentioned that his current employer had organized a team conversation when a recent homophobic hate crime had shaken several employees. Leon wanted to know if that would have been welcome at this company, or if it would be discouraged under the "we don't dwell on feelings" part of its job posting.

Jamie brought the issue to her partners, and at their weekly team meeting, Chana and Lane discussed what they would do about social issues as their team expanded. Leon's question was a good one and something they hadn't considered. They tried to think about how they could encourage that kind of discourse at work without it slowing down the pace that was a point of pride. They decided to tell Leon that, yes, that kind of discussion would be welcome at work, but they would facilitate it in a way that was authentic to their fast-paced, impact-driven culture. For example, Jamie explained to Leon, they might do it while in transit when they could drive and talk. The point was, Jamie said, that they would encourage him to be himself and collaboratively contribute to this very busy, focused, and competitive team. Leon liked that response and, after a few more interviews, was offered the job, which he accepted.

Jamie was pleased that their operational rigor was not going to be diluted by the focus on culture. Instead, she saw how it actually helped her recruit people who could fit into the intensity of the company.

Lane the Chief Financial Officer

Summary

- *Mindset:* I need to view our culture as a driver of business value.
- *Goal:* I can frame investor remarks around culture.

Lane thought of culture as a priority they would eventually "graduate" to focusing on. She felt that it was a luxury to talk about values and behaviors and that this startup should not spend time or money on anything that wasn't necessary. They had to focus solely on business-critical items. Specifically, they needed to successfully close their next round of funding. However, this new-hire debacle had been so costly to them because of wasted time that she was intrigued to think more creatively about how their culture could help them do business more effectively.

She decided to ask a venture-capitalist friend if he ever asked about culture when considering funding decisions. She shot off an email:

> Devan,
>
> Our group has recently defined our purpose, values, and behaviors. My initial reaction was to write this off as a silly exercise, but I recently saw how having these items explicitly stated helped us quickly identify and hire a strong candidate for an open role.
>
> You know well all the items on my "to-do list" as CFO of a startup, so I want your candid response: Do you care about culture when making funding decisions?
>
> Talk soon,
> Lane

Lane received a six-word response that read, "Yes—culture and performance are linked." This gave Lane an idea on how to restructure her remarks to funders: talk about performance with culture as a storytelling tool. She started noting which numbers would demonstrate their stated behaviors in action:

We measure twice and cut once: COGS, operating expenses
We are minimalists—in our processes with our spending and
    with ourselves: Capitalized expenses, SG&A, lease rentals

We move fast and don't dwell on failures or feelings: Revenue,
   operating income

Lane wanted to start thinking about how their cultural attributes could help them make stronger financial wins in each territory. Then the financial story would be differentiated during the
funding rounds; instead of just going number by number, which
they could still do with rigor, they would also talk about the people
behind those numbers.

· · ·

These snapshots provide a hypothetical overview of how different
roles each have responsibilities in meeting the evolved expectations of today's workforce. Yes, these summaries are a bit reductive
of the actual process it takes to do this work, but they are inspired
by conversations and people who are doing this work right now
in their companies. Some are being scrappy about this, like Lane
the startup CFO. That's perfectly appropriate in that case, given
that culture work can look different depending on the maturity of
a business. What we would caution against, however, is kicking
the "culture can" down the road and saying that the team will get
to it later; it can be hard for a startup to reverse unproductive or
nonstrategic behaviors once they have become routine. Others are
launching extensive commitments within established organizations, like Dave the CEO. He and others in similar situations need
to think about how to rally their teams to apply the strong skills
they already have to a new type of business problem and explain
to them the business case for culture—notably, that this work will

provide value to teams and accelerate the business strategy, bucking any misperception that culture-related initiatives are a distraction from "real work."

The takeaway from exploring these two markedly different scenarios is to see that culture work is scalable and that there are things you can do to move the work forward regardless of the maturity of your business, the seniority of your role, or the level of widespread buy-in across the organization. To reiterate again: this is the work of all of us.

5

A New Angle to Finding Personal Purpose at Work: Making the World a Better Place

Business executives have always been leaders of change in society, even when government is at the forefront. For instance, in 1987, labor secretary William Brock commissioned the Workforce 2000 study, which explored the competitive landscape in America, including risks and opportunities for the nation's growth in the next decade. Secretary Brock noted that the final research report highlighted urgent economic and labor trends that, taken together, made clear the business case for diversity as a means to continued economic competitiveness in America.

Today, which kind of case to make for diversity, or whether to make one at all, is debatable—but the point we wish to highlight is that government and business have long worked together to raise awareness and address social tensions and realities that have business and economic implications.[1]

Society is facing several enormous challenges, as we have in the past, with some of today's challenges looming as literal existential crises, like climate change. The way to address our twenty-first-century problems and leverage our opportunities is the way America has addressed challenges or innovated to take hold of opportunities for more than two hundred years: business and government have to collaborate and cooperate to advance society to where it needs to be next.

The Business Roundtable is a fifty-year-old association of the CEOs of the largest companies in America. Together, member companies of the Business Roundtable employ 20 million people, invest $226 billion annually in research and development, make $9 billion in charitable contributions, have an average collective stock-market capitalization of $18 trillion, and generate revenues of more than $9 trillion.[2] Think of any household or common brand name, and it is likely that the CEO of the company is a member of the Business Roundtable. This is a powerful group that influences, if not directs, the agenda in business worldwide. Several years ago, almost two hundred member CEOs came together and announced that the Roundtable was overturning a twenty-two-year-old belief and policy of the organization and pivoting from the idea that the purpose of a corporation is to maximize *shareholder value* to a new belief that the purpose of a corporation is to maximize *stakeholder value*.

With the focus and purpose of corporations having shifted from primarily shareholder value to shared values—with benefits to all stakeholders—workplace culture has become recognized as a critical asset to companies. Additionally, some of the power previously enshrined at the top of companies has been distributed throughout organizations because that is what the times and the general public call for and expect. With this shift, the workplace has become more like the town square, and culture—especially at the team level—has become more like how the school classroom used to be. It is a space in which people come together and learn new ideas, meet new people, and have their minds expanded.

As all these factors converge, the new most powerful group in corporations are people managers. They are the leaders who have to sharpen their skills to manage teams and keep work productive, fulfilling, inspiring, and engaging while allowing diverse groups of employees to reflect and express their true selves and their personal beliefs, even when those differ from the majority of their teammates or the manager herself.

This leads us to consider this new path to personal purpose at work for managers. Traditionally, people have not necessarily strived to become a manager in the same way that one might strive to become a CEO, physician, attorney, or famous entertainer. In other words, the idea of becoming a people manager hasn't typically been discussed as a pinnacle career achievement or an end goal. Usually, people have become managers on the way to another role to which they aspired or because they had to take on people-management responsibilities in order to earn more money and be promoted.

Today, the demands and deep impacts of managing people have risen to a level that requires personal purpose. Managers of today need to become managers of people not as a cursory or transient role but as an end unto itself. Managers have an opportunity to literally shape the future of society in America and beyond by shaping the mindsets and behaviors of the people they lead. By thinking and acting as much like community leaders as they do business leaders, managers have an opportunity to use the trust and influence bestowed on them to help people grow beyond limitations that might otherwise stay in place.

A Duke University and University of Arizona study found that the number of people who say they have nobody with whom they can discuss important matters had doubled.[3] The US Department of Health and Human Services reported research indicating that poor social connection can increase the risk of premature death by more than 60 percent.[4]

With people seeking connection more than ever and reporting that, outside of their closest family and friends, the next place they seek connection and community—more than with their next-door neighbors, at a religious organization, or anywhere else—is at work, it is clear how much of a role a manager can play in people's development.

The skills we need to design and manage purposeful, fulfilling, high-performing workplace cultures today are the very skills necessary in broader society to soften the toxic political rancor that has contributed to deep and harmful polarization around the world. These skills are also necessary to find solutions to the problems we face, like mass gun violence and environmental pollution, including contaminated water in large municipalities. These are the skills that can lead to a continuous decrease in systemic and structural racism, classism, and gender discrimination as well as an increase in human rights and the will to protect those rights no matter how often the party and leaders at the head of executive and legislative government bodies change.

The job of the manager is different today. It is the job that requires the *most* skill in a corporation. Managers have to understand the components of business—that's the finance, technology, operations, customer service, marketing and communications, legal compliance, administrative, and HR requirements. Yet they have the toughest job of all because they must also understand people. This is no longer as simple as following the golden rule of "doing unto others as you would have them do unto you." It requires cultural competency, empathy, high levels of emotional intelligence and maturity, and finding a balance between exhibiting strong confidence and a humble spirit.

What a manager might prefer for themselves is not at all what some of their employees would prefer. Where senior executives have to understand the business, provide resources, and set winning strategies in motion, they do not have to directly lead and shape dozens or hundreds of people. While a board of directors is responsible for keeping its nose in the business of the organization, it is required to keep its hands out. And whereas individual contributors are responsible only for making sure they are delivering what they are personally tasked to provide to the team, managers are responsible for everything. They must implement executive leadership's strategic imperatives. They must keep their noses, hands, and ears in the business. And they must deliver their own contributions while ensuring that everyone on their team is doing the same, and that often requires handling some kind of problem, challenge, or risk each week or even each day. Nobody else in today's corporations has as complex a job as a manager does when it comes to business performance and carrying the mantle to ensure an impactful, effective workplace culture.

Today, people should consider two things when stepping into a manager role: (1) Do they specifically want the job of shepherding, developing, and coaching people and creating an inclusive environment in which their people can thrive and grow into better, more mature, skilled, and capable versions of themselves? And (2) are they willing to invest their time into building or sharpening the skills required to be a great manager in a world that needs leaders who work to understand and care about *all* people as whole humans?

After all, today's employees, especially newly minted corporate professionals, will tell you: "I don't just work here." They are at work for a paycheck, yes, but, importantly to them, they are also there for greater purpose. You, as their manager, will be at your best and happiest if you, too, are not just there to work but also to help people build better skills and stronger character. By doing so, you are literally creating the conditions for a better workplace culture and a better societal culture, which eventually will lead to a better world.

Let's discuss the specific skills you will need to elevate to this new level of management leadership.

Workplace
Culture Skills

6

The Design of Valuable Communication

It is a basic and long-established expectation that business managers and rising leaders within organizations will be effective communicators. Nevertheless, the data show that employees feel that most managers underperform when it comes to communicating.[1]

The existing lack of skill makes it even more critical to pay attention to communication—particularly as it relates to redesigning or refining a company's culture to be responsive to new needs and expectations in the workplace. The communication skills that have allowed managers to navigate and sufficiently lead workplaces in the past, with a focus on the working human, *are not* a match for the workplace culture and communication needs of today, given the expectations of the whole human.

Consider this: traditionally, communication challenges that impact workplace culture have been issues of *clarity* and *compliance*. However, the newer communication challenges impacting workplace culture are around topics related to *identity* and *values*— as more employees seek purpose, societal change, and greater self-expression. Let's get into the precise differences between these two types of communications. Clarity and compliance communication issues stem from people not knowing or understanding the work they are to do or the related processes and practices. This includes:

- What work employees should be doing
- How to do the work
- How quickly the work should be done
- Who employees should turn to for help with work
- Whether it is okay for any employee to ask for help
- The proper processes or policies for approvals of work or extensions of deadlines
- What to do when someone, regardless of level, is not complying with processes or policies
- The standard and definition of quality and success
- The details or process for compensation or recognition when work is done well
- What rights, options, or power employees have regarding their work and how it is done

In industries where work is heavily process oriented, like manufacturing, there is often tremendous communication around the specifics of the work to do and standards for how it should be done, but there can be greater challenges in compliance. This points to a need for more communication along with operational changes.

You can probably think of an example from the news media or from direct experience within an organization of a culture problem that resulted from ongoing failures to communicate and reiterate clear direction to employees and help them understand how to comply with expectations—and what to do to hold others accountable for the same. Clarity and compliance communication issues tend to be about the work.

Let's turn our attention now to the other category we are focused on here: identity and values. Communication issues related to these topics can arise when people feel a real or perceived threat—or experience an injury—to their identity or values or both. Past social and workplace culture norms created what could be sometimes described as an artificial environment—comprised of people with similar beliefs, or people pretending to have such. Since employees were thought to have the same values, checked their feelings at the door when reporting to work, dressed and presented themselves according to formal or socially enforced policies, it was a rule that divisive topics or beliefs were off limits for discussion. Managers and team members did not need communications skills or language to create safe, inclusive spaces for everyone to be themselves and express themselves.

But now, given the shift in employee expectations we've outlined in previous chapters, there is increased likelihood that people are going to need or want communication on:

- Why it seems the same "type" of people get promoted or recognized (and the attributes of the "type" seem irrelevant to readiness or deservedness for promotion or recognition)
- What to do when some employees seem open and accepting of everyone except coworkers with particular characteristics
- Whether it is okay to express disappointment or satisfaction with developments from the judiciary and/or legislative branches of government, and why or why not
- Whether it is acceptable to be openly upset and affected by news reports of violence in general or violence against a person or people because of who they are, and why or why not
- What it means for a person's career and trajectory at this organization if they prefer to work only the generally accepted full-time work hours of forty hours per week and do so in a remote or hybrid work model
- What it means for a person's career at this organization if they would prefer not attending social events or would rather only attend social events within workday hours
- Whether it is okay to be up-front and vocal about one's political or social beliefs, even when a person seems to be the only one who has a given perspective—and whether a manager will validate and reinforce the acceptableness of the person sharing their views, and why or why not
- Whether it is okay to express, and how to express, strong and unpopular personal opinions such as the idea that certain types or groups of people seem to be treated in special ways

Note the differences in the two categories of communications needs. Whereas clarity and compliance communication issues are typically about the work, identity and values communication issues tend to be about the workers (which affects the work, too). The tools and tactics to address these two categories of communication and culture problems are different. Thus, developing or maintaining a high-impact workplace culture in today's context requires transforming the communications skills of leaders and the entire team.

In this climate, it is healthiest and most helpful to see every issue or problem as an opportunity to learn more and advance or fortify the culture and the business. With that mindset, let's talk about a few ways to apply or enhance communications skills to make gains that address contemporary needs.

Solving Clarity and Compliance Communication Issues

Clarity and compliance communication problems are challenges that arise when people are confused about some aspect of their work, how to get it done, and how to be accountable and hold others accountable for success and the commensurate rewards.

These issues can be in full force impacting a culture but still overlooked because they are the kinds of issues that people raise once or twice and then complain about less frequently or more quietly because they later accept that these issues are just the way things are. If it becomes too unbearable, they simply look for another job.

To find and address these problems, a leader can review existing employee survey data, collect new employee survey data, or have informal conversations with team members to see if there are indications or outright declarations that communication is a problem. When complaints are candid and straightforward, it is simple to identify the problem, but indicators that poor communication skills are getting in the way of culture and team performance can also be subtle and difficult to discern. Sometimes team members talk about the symptoms or experience they are having and never use the word "communication." Key words and phrases that may be indicative of a clarity and compliance communication problem include:

1. I don't understand how to . . .
2. I am confused when . . .
3. I am not sure what to prioritize when . . .
4. I am hearing conflicting information from . . .
5. I don't know what to say to my colleague or manager when . . .
6. I am not sure when I am expected to . . .
7. I think there has been a change, but nobody has said anything about . . .
8. I'm not sure if I'm doing well on my work or potential promotion because . . .
9. I get assigned more work, but I'm not a part of the decisions regarding . . .
10. Nobody ever asks me . . .

Following up when you hear these phrases could reveal clarity and compliance communication problems that you can address immediately because they fall within the purview of traditional management and culture challenges. For instance, it is common in some workplaces for high performers to be overutilized while average or poor performers are less utilized or underutilized. After all, everyone knows that asking the high performers to complete projects will lead to great results. Consider if a manager heard in their conversation with an employee, "I am not sure what to prioritize during busy season when I am asked by multiple managers to complete more than one project. I get stressed and worried, so I work every weekend to get all the projects done quickly so none of the managers will get behind or be upset, but I am starting to feel anxious all the time and burnt out."

In addition to the need to discontinue the behavior of overloading high performers, we can infer from this scenario that inadequate communication is likely a problem since the employee describes uncertainty about expectations and priorities—in other words, the employee has a lack of clarity. The employee's chronic feelings of anxiety and burnout are certainly shaping their perception of culture and could be part of their conversation with other employees as well. There are several actions that can be taken and pieces of information that could be clearly communicated to reduce or eliminate the recurrence of this experience for this employee and others.

For example, managers could be proactive when making assignments and communicate to the employee the order in which to add their project and complete all assigned projects. Managers could communicate to employees that if they have received so many assignments that they feel compelled to work during their off hours, they should talk to assigning managers about clear and graduated deadlines and priority of projects. As another example, managers could change the process so that assignments route through only the employee's direct manager, who will always know their workload and be able to help them prioritize; then, managers could communicate this new process to all employees. It could also be communicated to employees that if a manager or other leader forgets or is unaware of the process and makes a project request directly, the employee is empowered to ask the requester to speak with their manager. These formal surveys or informal conversations are tools, and the sample solutions are tactics that could solve this and other clarity and compliance communication problems.

Solving Identity and Values Communication Issues

Identity and values communication challenges can emerge when people sense an imposition on their identity or values; these issues are more likely to result in tension, frustration, and anger. However, the tendency to react so intensely can be tempered over time with new skills. Also, the very nature of the issues raised in this category may mean that conversations and follow-up support to address a problem may not fully solve the core problem because many of these issues originate from societal systems, historical precedent, and deeply socialized beliefs that are not easily changed. Therefore, part of communicating well regarding identity and values issues is acknowledging the impact of the core problem or tension and *allowing time and space for people to process* while noting that the manager or team will need to rescope the problem to something that can be solved, acted upon, or accepted within the context of the organization and team.

To identify identity and values communication issues, managers can ask employees about their experiences via surveys or informal conversations; they can also ask leaders on the team to engage in these conversations. It is also possible that managers will not have to ask because, with employees growing more vocal and activist, these issues may be reported or shared proactively and organically. To address these issues, managers might create and communicate new policies and rules or develop and launch new mindset and behavioral norms with the team.

Before we move on to solutions, let's name the barriers we're up against and why this subcategory of communication can be so difficult. Many of the various barriers can be summed up in one word: *anxiety.*

Managers and coworkers are hesitant to communicate on these issues because of many anxieties rooted in how we perceive others and our worries about how they might perceive us. Some of the ones we have commonly heard in our work include:

- If I share how I really feel, my team might think I am ignorant or out of touch.
- I need to give my coworker or employee feedback about their work, but they are the only person of their identity on the team; what if they think my feedback is motivated by bias rather than performance?
- I might use the wrong words to express my opinion; what if I come across offensively?

- What if I do a fine job providing feedback but my coworker or employee does not react well because they simply do not like feedback?
- What if my coworker or employee holds a grudge after I share how I really feel about a topic or their performance and it affects our relationship and future interactions?
- What if my coworker or employee appears okay with the conversation we had but I later learn they have been gossiping about what we discussed and creating bitterness and negativity with other team members?
- What if I sense or see bias and fragility in this person's comments and behaviors but it seems that they have low self-awareness?

Conversational receptiveness and *feedback receptiveness* are two advanced communication skills managers and teams can work on to increase communications performance to build the competences and trust that can be leveraged to overcome specific anxieties that may come up later.

Conversational receptiveness was established through research by Michael Yeomans and Julia Minson, scientists at Imperial College and the Harvard Kennedy School, who found that people can use language to communicate "willingness to thoughtfully engage with opposing views."[2] In their studies, they used both human evaluators and a machine learning algorithm to identify the types of conversation cues that make a person seem more or less receptive to the viewpoints of someone who they know is on the opposite side of an issue. Importantly, they also identified the conversational elements that can make escalation less likely. The

THE DESIGN OF VALUABLE COMMUNICATION

"receptiveness recipe" they developed based on the research data, which included a field experiment with working professionals, is:

- Positive statements rather than negations
- Explicit acknowledgment of understanding
- Finding points of agreement
- Hedging to soften claims

The data showed that executives who were rated as more receptive were considered better teammates, advisors, and workplace representatives and were seen as more desirable partners for future collaboration; their messages were also seen as more persuasive.

Nathan Fulham and Kori Krueger, scientists at Carnegie Mellon University, studied receptivity to feedback and found that three key barriers to people being able to accept feedback are:[3]

- Threats to the feedback recipient's sense of self
- Distrust of the feedback or feedback giver
- Beliefs about the feedback recipient's willingness or ability to change

To get the most out of these skills, teams need opportunities to practice and build trust by communicating in low-stakes situations before they are tackling more emotionally charged issues together. Starting with building a team norm of giving and receiving honest feedback and focusing on the behavior, not the person, is a good place to begin the work of communicating at a higher level together. To do this, we like the "Conversations That Matter" tool,[4] developed by The Ohio State University. It's a helpful structure that managers and teams can use to engage in effective conversations. The framework is:

- Clarify the topic
- Explore the options
- Commit to actions

Consider the following key points as you think about how to apply the framework.

Part I: Clarify the Topic

Conversations with your team can range from joyous and motivating topics to sad, disappointing, or anger-inducing ones. Regardless of the tone and focus of the conversation, it is helpful to start by clarifying the topics to be discussed. It is common for people to have a lot to say when they are experiencing heightened emotions, and it can be challenging for people to be clear and concise, whether they are emoting or not. Therefore, quickly outlining what will be discussed helps you and participants in the conversation focus their minds and also makes it easier to identify when the conversation has veered off topic.

Part II: Explore the Options

While it is true that some conversations at work are for simple enjoyment with no goal or next step attached, more often there is a reason for connecting even when a colleague is discussing a personal matter. Therefore, it is helpful to think of the second part of the conversation as the time to explore options.

Your value during this part of the conversation is in asking great questions that help your colleague(s) consider a full range of possibilities. When deciding what we can do to solve a problem, leverage an opportunity, or move forward in a situation, it is normal for availability and recency biases to get in the way; this is the tendency to think that only the ideas we have come up with so far are the best way to proceed because they are most "available" or recent examples in our mind, making the approach feel vivid, familiar, and right.

Part III: Commit to Actions

After setting up a clear conversation topic and thinking expansively about options, the final part of the conversation is to commit to actions. Depending on the nature of the conversation, you might find that these actions are small and simple, but don't confuse small with insignificant—sometimes the value of a conversation is simply to process what we are feeling or thinking, and the next action may be to commit to moving on mentally. Grudges and resentment have real and negative consequences in the workplace, so a conversation that simply leads to acceptance is powerful and important.

Follow-up actions could also be about moving a project forward, completing a task, or launching a new initiative. Just be sure that whether the next step is minor or major, you conclude the conversation by being very specific about what will happen, by when, and by whom. Of course, this can be informal—you and your colleagues can simply note on paper (or even just mentally) what is to happen next. Or it can be more formal, with a follow-up email or notation about the action items and related due dates.

Putting It All Together

In her TED Talk on "10 Ways to Have a Better Conversation,"[5] author and radio journalist Celeste Headlee—a professional interviewer who has made her living over twenty years conversing with thousands of people ranging from truck drivers, to Nobel prize winners, to kindergarten teachers, to billionaire business leaders—says, "It used to be that to have a polite conversation, we just had to follow the advice of Henry Higgins in *My Fair Lady* and stick to the weather and your health. But these days, with climate change and anti-vaxxing, those subjects are not safe, either."

Headlee goes on to make the point that in today's world, things have become so contentious that any and every conversation is at risk of resulting in a bitter argument. At the same time, 60 percent of workers ages eighteen to thirty-four "feel their employers should train employees on how to have constructive debates about these issues inside and outside of the workplace."[6] As a manager, you are in a position to grow in the area of communications around all issues, but especially issues related to identity and values, and help your people graduate to a new level of communication skills that will support a purposeful culture.

7

The Mechanics of Listening

I n his popular Entrepreneurial Selling™ course, Northwestern Kellogg School of Management Clinical Professor of Marketing Craig Wortmann teaches students to ask themselves a focused question as they approach the entrance of every cocktail party in their career, and that question is: "Am I working?" If the answer is yes, then Professor Wortmann implores you to approach the duration of the event with great strategic intent, and his class goes into the precise details of what you should do. He gets into specifics along the lines of:

- Practicing the quick *script* you should say when you march up to key people in the room and stick out your hand in introduction
- Creating a Story Matrix™, a list of stories you have drafted and subsequently committed to memory so that you have a

relevant story to rattle off no matter where the person with whom you're networking takes the conversation

- Devising an *exit strategy*, a warm line that is particularly helpful if you want to extract yourself from a conversation so that you can keep working the room, never lingering too long with one person or group (after all, core to working is working the full room)
- Managing a *database* of all your contacts so that the minute the party ends, you can pull up your file and enter the contact information and personal stories that you discussed with each person you met; this way, you can follow up with them with a personalized note

Professor Wortmann walks through this level of detail so that his students can truly maximize every cocktail party—and his students eagerly scribble down notes on his highly practical and engaging tips and tricks. However, he also notes that if the answer is "no" to the original "Am I working?" question, then you should go ahead and do whatever you want: ditch the Story Matrix™ and chat about the weather; forgo any exit strategy and talk to the same person all night if you want to. And he says this with deep sincerity. If meeting new people isn't fun for you and you're not working, then don't anxiously work the room—enjoy yourself instead. If you want to hover near the bar and catch the end of the baseball game on TV—and you're not working—then go for it, Professor Wortmann encourages. The point is, recognize why you're at the party and scale your approach accordingly.

The same goes for listening. *Harvard Business Review* researchers Rebecca D. Minehart, Benjamin B. Symon, and

Laura K. Rock published a piece titled "What's Your Listening Style?"[1] that argues we should recognize *why* we are listening in any given scenario before beginning the act itself. The style with which you should listen can be scaled to the type of conversation you encounter. This is important, the researchers report, because the "default way we listen" may not be productive to all our goals. For example, your default style might be what they term that of an "analytical listener"—focused on picking apart a problem—but the situation might instead call for a "relational listener," one ready to advance relationship building and listen with emotional empathy. Or you might be what they've listed as a "critical listener"—committed to evaluating "both the content of the conversations and the reliability of the speaker themselves." And there is a fourth type, the "task-focused listener," who prioritizes efficient communication.

If you're in a work situation and your analytical-listener style shows up for a conversation that calls for a relational listener, the right type of listening won't take place. The analytical style might pepper someone with who-, what-, where-, and when-type questions, and the respondent—who was looking to share personal stories and build a connection—very well might shut down and share little information at all. In that situation, both members of the conversation may grow frustrated. The analytical listener doesn't get the information she craves, and her conversation partner may feel alienated or, even worse, disrespected.

Using Professor Wortmann's disciplined approach to cocktail parties as inspiration, we really should train ourselves to ask, "Am I an analytical, relational, critical, or task-focused listener in this situation?" and then scale the conversational approach accordingly. Doing this well means mastering all four listening styles and properly diagnosing which style will be most effective for any given scenario.

How to Actually Listen

Diagnosing an issue is one thing, but progressing with the actual treatment plan is an entirely different remit. Therefore, once you have done the good work of recognizing which type of listener is best suited for your situation (the equivalent to answering Professor Wortmann's "Am I working?" question), you should feel like you have the objective for your conversation clearly laid out before you. That's what we find so helpful about the four types outlined above. You are listening with [fill in the blank] intention.

That means you're ready to actually start listening, but what does one do to effectively listen (the equivalent of Professor Wortmann's very specific tips on *how* to work a room)? Seth S. Horowitz wrote a 2012 opinion column in the *New York Times* titled "The Science and Art of Listening."[2] In it, he makes the argument that *attention* is a key capability in listening. He details the neurological process of paying attention and specifies the difference between *hearing* and *listening*. I'm sure you can think of an instance in which you heard someone talking (as in, you were aware that someone was speaking) but were distracted or disinterested and didn't pay attention—and therefore didn't retain anything that was said. Happens to us all the time.

Paying attention requires incredible discipline. Perhaps the best way to understand this point is to attend a hot-yoga course. Consider this: You enter a 105-degree room that registers at 40 percent humidity. Sweat beads immediately form across your forehead and, within minutes, there is a stream of moisture running down your back. The instructor puts ninety minutes on the clock and begins leading you through a range of spine-twisting, gravity-defying poses. Each one seems harder than the last—arms sideways, hips thrust back, one leg planted on the floor, the other pointed up to the ceiling. You attempt each as puddles of sweat form on your yoga mat. Then, finally, the instructor says that for the next pose, "Savasana," you need to lie down on your back, arms by your sides, legs out straight. Essentially, you're simply lying on the floor. *Whew*, you think, *this break is much needed!* But then the instructor has the audacity to say that this pose is actually the hardest one of all. What? How could that be? The point of this pose is to stay entirely present. To just think about your breath—no thoughts wandering to your grocery list, the emails waiting in your inbox, the song lyrics stuck in your head, none of that. You have to pay attention to your breath instead. And that is, for many, a very hard thing to do.

To actually pay attention when you're supposed to be listening, keep these guidelines in mind:

- If you're going to be sitting while meeting with someone, select a chair that doesn't face a window or door. Seeing people walk by is hugely distracting. The virtual equivalent of this is to hide the view you have of yourself on Teams, Zoom, etc. Looking at ourselves takes our mind off of who we're supposed to be listening to.
- Put your phone down—face down—so that you don't see the alerts coming in.

- Look your conversation partner in the eyes, and if that's awkward for you, look at the spot just above the bridge of their nose; to them, it will feel like you're making eye contact.
- After a key point, try to say back what you just heard them say to be sure you're hearing them correctly.
- If you notice your mind starting to wander, practice the discipline of refocusing on the conversation; you are essentially in a Savasana situation. It can be hard to stay present, but with practice and the elimination of distractions, paying attention becomes a core business skill.

How Managers and Teams Can Avoid Listening Pitfalls

Professor Wortmann doesn't just teach students what good business interactions look like; he's also a deeply funny and theatrical professor who reenacts some terrible business interactions, too. The genius of this is that students leave his class not only with the frameworks for what to do but also with a vivid memory of what to avoid. With that construct in mind, and while you're working to master the four listening types and the discipline of paying attention, let's also consider what bad listening looks like. McKinsey published a snapshot of what not to do as part of its "executive's guide to better listening" by Bernard T. Ferrari.[3] In it, there is an overview of six archetypes of bad listeners, and using these as a guide, we can understand what bad listening looks like in the context of the new expectations of employees. The archetypes that Ferrari presents are:

The Opinionator

- *What Ferrari says about this archetype:* "The Opinionator listens to others primarily to determine whether or not their ideas conform to what he or she already believes to be true."

- *Our take on how to manage this impulse:* Sure, you may have a hypothesis ahead of talking to someone, and you may rightfully want to prove or disprove your hypothesis, but avoid being an Opinionator by setting aside any leading questions. Try to draw inspiration from a savvy researcher who certainly has a hypothesis ahead of entering data collection but would never ask questions that lead a data subject to know what that hypothesis is. Instead, strike a neutral tone and ask, "Why do you think that?" instead of "Well, I think that this happened; why do you agree or disagree?"

The Grouch

- *What Ferrari says about this archetype:* "Grouches are . . . blocked by a feeling of certainty that your idea is wrong."

- *Our take on how to manage this impulse:* Watch your body language; Grouches can be relentless about rolling their eyes or sharing a blatant look of disgust. There is nothing wrong with bringing a healthy skepticism to a conversation, but try to relax your facial muscles and present a neutral tone and posture so that the person with whom you're conversing doesn't just shut down from any perceived (or real) negativity.

The Preambler

- *What Ferrari says about this archetype:* "The Preambler's windy lead-ins and questions are really stealth speeches, often intended to box conversation partners into a corner."
- *Our take on how to manage this impulse:* Let someone else start the conversation; if you have trouble harnessing your verbal contributions up front, then perhaps frame the meeting in your head as someone else's; it's for them to run and for you to . . . listen to. If they ask for your opinion, perhaps engage the line "I want to hear you out first, so I'll save my comments for the end." Then, jot down notes on what you want to say when it's your turn.

The Perseverator

- *What Ferrari says about this archetype:* "Perseverators talk a lot without saying anything. If you pay close attention to one of these poor listeners, you'll find that their comments and questions don't advance the conversation."
- *Our take on how to manage this impulse:* Try to become comfortable with the lines "I don't know" and "I'll have to think about that." The pressure to always seem like an expert can rush some people to talk when they really don't have anything substantive to say. There is great power in saying that you don't know. It creates space for genuine listening.

The Answer Man

- *What Ferrari says about this archetype:* "Answer Man spouts solutions before there is even a consensus about the challenge—a clear signal that input from conversation partners isn't needed."

- *Our take on how to manage this impulse:* See the earlier advice regarding the Preambler. Try to write down your thoughts instead of cutting in on a conversation. And perhaps frame your point of view as "Have you considered . . ." instead of "You should do . . ." This positions your idea as an option for them to react to instead of the "right" thing to do.

The Pretender

- *What Ferrari says about this archetype:* "Pretenders feign engagement and even agreement but either aren't interested in what you're saying or have already made up their minds."
- *Our take on how to manage this impulse:* Remind yourself that humans expect reciprocity—"Treat me the way you expect me to treat others." Therefore, if you are merely pretending to care about someone or something, then be ready for other people to similarly pretend around you. If you don't want the workplace to devolve into a charade where everyone is just acting, then ditch this archetype and be a person of your word.

Top Takeway on Listening

If you take one thing away from this chapter, it should be that intention and attention are essential to be a good listener. We live in a world that thrives off of—or even demands—multitasking, but our experience is that we are not actually very good at such a skill and that multitasking can backfire when you're trying to manage the new expectations of workplace culture. Instead, we need to commit to listening—truly listening—when it's needed. For that, we must explicitly express intent. Tell yourself, "I am listening right now," and then do precisely that.

8

The Nuts and Bolts of Empathy

ndrew Alexander King is a global explorer, entrepreneur, and outdoor athlete who was born in Detroit, Michigan, and has climbed more than fifty mountains around the world, including the highest mountains in the Atlantic, Indian, and Pacific Oceans, as well as Mount Kilimanjaro—the highest peak on the African continent. He is the founder of the Between Worlds Project, a company that brings together people and organizations across geographic continents and cultures to develop and advance solutions for some of the most entrenched challenges humankind faces, such as gender discrimination and climate change. King posted a wise, insightful, poetic thought on Instagram—apparently informed by his collaboration with different kinds of people from all over the world—and it speaks in simple eloquence to the essence of empathy, which is the ability and willingness to see and feel from another person's perspective:[1]

> *I'm pretty sure*
> *There isn't one person you have met*
> *you wouldn't have love for*
> *If you stopped and got to know their*
> *whole true story of life*
> *And willingly lived a day or lifetime in their shoes*
> *To understand how they truly see*
> *and step into each day*

Psychological and social scientists have established that there are three kinds of empathy: emotional empathy, cognitive empathy, and empathic concern. Dr. Jamil Zaki, a social neuroscientist at Stanford, says having one piece without the others can lead to different outcomes in the workplace.[2] Therefore, while each of these three expressions of empathy is useful, together they produce a holistic and substantive experience for those who encounter a manager or leader who has activated triple empathy.

So what does this mean for the workplace? Managers who have emotional empathy are adept at understanding how their colleagues are feeling, and they create a sense of closeness and connection, inspiring their teams to act with empathy, too, by modeling it from the top. Managers who have cognitive empathy take perspective and think about and imagine what it must be like for a colleague in general or to be in a particular situation a coworker or employee may be facing. Managers who show empathic concern take action to ensure their colleagues know and feel they are cared for and have support when facing a challenge. Each of these expressions of empathy imparts something different and, with awareness, can show up in helpful ways within workplace culture, especially in today's new context and in light of new expectations of leadership when it comes to cultivating meaningful conversations and a sense of purpose.

I'm Not the Empathetic Type—It's Just Not My Style!

Reading these details about the definitions of empathy can cause people to reflect on whether they are empathetic, which then can often lead to one of three typical conclusions: people either think they are cut out for empathic management and leadership or are already leading in this way, they believe empathic leadership is too difficult and not for them, or they have concerns that leading with empathy will negatively affect the performance of an entire business unit.

Some managers worry that empathic leadership will result in a group of weak and ineffective team members or will create an environment where the manager is always dealing with people's excuses for not performing their best and constantly having to play counselor, therapist, parental figure, or cheerleader to someone on their team each day. In short, empathy as a leading characteristic can be less popular because it can seem at odds with the demands of a high-performing organization, or it can result in experiences that feel phony or disingenuous to some people depending on their personality.

Consider this perspective on how empathy is a skill that can be built, starting with framing and perceiving it as a strength rather than a personal or organizational weakness.

As an example, let's turn to the US Marines, one of the most tough-minded and hard-nosed organizations in the world. The Marines have an acronym that serves as a mnemonic to help members of the corps remember the organization's primary leadership values and principles; the acronym does not forthrightly state empathy, but the idea of empathy is implied in nearly half of the stated principles.[3] The acronym is JJDIDTIEBUCKLE, and it stands for justice, judgment, dependability, initiative, decisiveness, tact, integrity, endurance, bearing, unselfishness, courage, knowledge, loyalty, and enthusiasm.

Six of the principles—justice, initiative, unselfishness, courage, knowledge, and loyalty—correlate to the three-part view of empathy, where a person is able to connect with someone else's feelings, imagine how it must feel to be that person in a given situation, and act to show care and concern because there is a clear sense of how the other person feels.

While empathy is nuanced and implied within the core Marines leadership principles, some Marines actively advocate for it and say empathy should be explicitly stated within the core values because they see their colleagues acting with empathy every day. Referring to JJDIDTIEBUCKLE, one Marine quoted in a research study of the organization's leadership principles and behaviors said, "I would take out one of those Es and add empathy. Empathy is a thing that allows you to see things from other people's perspectives. It's not a touchy-feely thing where we have to . . . hug them and make sure they don't ever get hurt."[4] While this Marine's description may be too sharp for some people, his point is clear: empathy is about seeing a situation or experience, or trying to see it, the way your colleague does. The ways in which leaders at an organization choose to express empathy is a matter of style. For an organization whose job is to protect a nation, a tough-as-nails style is appropriate. For an organization whose job is to care for people who are ill and bring them back to wellness—like a hospital system, for example—a sensitive style of empathy is more fitting. Regardless of style, the empathy mindset and behavior can be activated and applied in any organization, and the style in which it is applied is based on the culture of the organization. This debunks the idea that empathy and strength are opposites. They can be one and the same.

Empathy grows stronger when people believe they are capable of it and practice it, and it grows weaker when they believe the opposite or are in environments where doubt and cynicism are norms. Dr. Carol Dweck, a psychologist known for developing the growth-mindset concept, conducted experiments with Dr. Zaki in which they found that people who think of empathy as a trait versus as a skill behave quite differently when situations that invite empathy arise. Those who believed it was a trait, and therefore something that you either have or don't, did not try as hard as those who believed it was a skill. It seemed that the trait-minded participants didn't want to be exposed for their lack of empathy if they fell short, so they didn't try very much to begin with. Conversely, the empathy-is-a-skill participants gave much more effort and "spent more time listening to the stories of people from different races and spent more energy to understand the opinions of people they disagreed with politically. They put effort into their empathy, because they believed that on the other side of that work was a version of themselves they wanted to be: someone who could connect with others more effectively."[5]

With the understanding that empathy is a skill and strength and does not require you to be a cheerleader unless that's your style and aligned with the culture of your organization, let's explore the best way to practice it.

How to Enact Empathy

Get to Know Each Person on Your Team

It sounds obvious, but we have learned in our work and seen in industry data that many leaders set out a direction for a team and give instructions on projects but rarely or never stop to talk with each member of their team to find out how that project resonates with them and relates to their personal career and ambitions. In a Gallup study of employees who had recently resigned from their employers, "more than half said that nobody—including their manager—had talked to them about how they were feeling in their role within the last three months; and 52 percent of exiting employees said there was something their manager or organization could have done to keep them in their job."[6]

If empathy is understanding a scenario or experience from another person's perspective and having a sense of how they feel, practicing it is easier if you know and understand details about why your colleagues are doing the work they do. Now, it's important to clarify that this does not mean that colleagues should expect to only do work they like, nor does it mean companies need to meet or surpass each individual preference; that's not the point here. We do believe fit matters, and sometimes people are quite frankly not a fit for a certain job, team, or company.

Following are a few of the basic questions to ask in an empathy-focused conversation—but really the key is to be or become genuinely interested in and curious about every person on your team. People don't just show up on a job; they are always there for a specific reason. The default conclusion is that people are there for a paycheck. Of course, people need to be paid, but people who are merely collecting a check rarely stay around for long. There is something else driving them to work, and even the motivation to work for a check has an underlying reason. Why do they need or want the check? Do they have a family to take care of? A goal they are pursuing? Student loans they need to pay off? A certain lifestyle to which they aspire, like traveling around the world every summer? Get to know and understand the motivators that drive your colleagues to do the work you all are doing, and with that understanding will come a greater understanding of each person. Notice that each of these potential reasons for working we've mentioned naturally lead to other questions, all of which result in you knowing more about each of your team members and what they value and how they see the world.

Consider if you know the answers to the following questions for everyone on your team—or at least everyone who reports to you:

- What made you interested in working here?
- How did you learn about the job?
- What do you like so far about the job?
- What do you dislike about the job?
- How would you describe our culture (at the enterprise level and team level)?

- How do you feel about our culture (at the enterprise level and team level)?
- Do you feel supported in the work you do?
- What would make you feel more supported in the work you do?
- What makes you feel motivated?
- What stresses you out?
- What are your dream projects and your ideal role? *(Note that these cannot be guaranteed but that you'd still like to know what their dream projects are so if the opportunity becomes available, you can position them for it.)*
- What projects and roles do you dread? *(Note that you cannot guarantee that they will always get to steer clear of these projects and roles but that you'd still like to know what they dread so you can position them, if possible and practical, to work on projects and in roles they prefer.)*
- Where do you see yourself going in your career in the next six to twelve months? What about in the next two years? What would you like to contribute to in order to help you prepare to reach those milestones?
- Feedback helps people grow, so I will give you feedback regularly. I want you to know that you can give me feedback as well. Are you accustomed to receiving direct and honest feedback? Are you accustomed to giving direct and honest feedback?
- What's your key focus as a person in general for the next year—in what way(s) do you want to be different, stronger, or better?

Create Empathy-Inducing Environments

Empathy seems to be predominantly about *people*, but let's not bypass the importance of the *environment*. Kurt Lewin, a pioneer of social and organizational psychology and an applied- and quantitative-psychology theorist, created a formula to describe human behavior and how it could be influenced:

$$B = f(P, E)$$

Behavior is a function of a person and their environment.

The validity of the formula has been proven in empirical research and can be observed in everyday life, including when it comes to empathy. The "E" in the equation—or environment—is essential. Consider this: The CEO of a company was known as a brilliant strategist, which is how he got the job. However, he developed a reputation for humiliating leaders in front of their peers, sometimes over substantive issues but often over minor points. He would also have meetings with individual leaders and assign them all the same project without informing the collective that they were all working on the same goal. Later, once the leaders and their teams submitted their work, he would compare their results and criticize the "losers" for not having done the project as well or as quickly as their colleagues. The chairman of the board didn't intervene with this CEO because he wanted to leverage his strategy chops to increase the company's sales and market cap.

Over time, the CEO's actions and board chairman's failure to reign in the CEO resulted in severe losses because managers at the corporate headquarters would hoard information and try to be the first to "win" with their leaders, who in turn were trying to "win" with the CEO. They spent so much time bitterly battling to be the first or the best that they did not provide proper support, materials, or updates to the field. Only after many misses on sales goals or new product launches would some managers or employees step forward to share what was happening or to report it anonymously. Even customers could feel the difference, and it was evident in customer feedback. The issues in this story seem evident now because it's all said and done. But rarely when leaders, employees, and companies are going through this kind of experience can they parse apart the issue.

In this case, the CEO's actions created an environment of criticism and cynicism. This turned into teams fighting each other, managers viewing one another with suspicion, and most employees totally checking out. A culture of deeply entrenched apathy set in. Employees did just enough work to keep their jobs, and as soon as they could find new jobs, they resigned. Sales plunged and attrition skyrocketed. Empathy had been completely stamped out.

The work environment can drive empathy or totally derail it. In the case of the company outlined above, new people were hired to replace the employees who were leaving every week, but once new entrants observed the apathy and bitter competition between teams, they resorted to one of these two strategies to remain "safe" as well, and neither path included empathy. Someone entering the organization with a can-do attitude and a will to win, both of which tap into empathy, would soon discard their usual behavior and adjust to survive and succeed within the environment. As a leader, pay attention to the kind of environment you are creating or succumbing to and do the work to ensure that empathy is at the core.

Give Honest and Frequent Feedback

A *Harvard Business Review* article cites data wherein 39 percent of employees said they regard the inability of their manager to provide constructive criticism as ineffective leadership.[7] Your team is looking for clear direction and corrective direction when needed. Fear of providing feedback is too common among managers, and it often comes from a good place. Some leaders who care about how their people feel do not want to be mean or be perceived as such, so they either do not give feedback or give it in such a sugarcoated or diplomatic way that the employee does not understand how they need to improve. Ironically, inauthentic, incomplete, or undelivered feedback is the opposite of empathy. People want to do well; employees want to do a good job. It is true that critical feedback is hard for some people to hear, especially if they are not used to receiving it, but it is harder for them to be overlooked for promotions, fired, or inadequately prepared for a future opportunity because they have not received the feedback necessary along the way to progress. The key to empathic feedback is to deliver it honestly, frequently, and with care. People can better receive feedback if you set the expectation that they are in an environment and on a team where feedback will be delivered, with an explanation as to why that is necessary. So do the conditioning necessary for people to be waiting or even asking for feedback and receptive to it, even if it is not exactly what they want to hear.

A few additional considerations for emphathic feedback:

- Be precise and clear with examples of what behaviors or skills need to be corrected and ideas for how they can be improved.
- Think of a story you can share if it feels right in the moment to ease some of the anxiety, anger, or tension.
- Become comfortable with intense emotions from others. That is part of the mantle of leadership and par for the course when you lead with empathy.

If you have asked these empathy-informing questions, have created an environment for empathy, and are delivering feedback frequently, people may say you are tough—but they will also say you care.

9

Decision Architecture

When the US Supreme Court voted to overturn *Roe v. Wade*, eliminating women's control of their bodies and reproductive rights overnight, many professionals across corporations were divided. Some supported the decision, and many vocally disapproved of it. This left both elected officials and business leaders reeling about what to say and whether to say anything at all. For many, the decision needed to take into consideration customer and investor perception and internal considerations— deciding whether they should reassure their employees that they would find a way to support them if they needed the healthcare services that had now been stripped away after fifty years.

Allstate CEO Tom Wilson was one of the leaders who has since spoken about the pressure of the moment, and we use his example in this chapter on decision architecture because he used a decision framework. At an Aspen Institute conference, Wilson discussed how he made such a decision.[1] He said he and his team created a "Societal Engagement Framework," the basis of which were the Allstate core values. Wilson said that whenever someone asks him and his team to take a stand or make a leadership decision on an issue, they can refer to the framework to determine if doing so would be "consistent with the way we run our business." He discussed several values-based filters that make up the framework:

1. Will this help us do a better job for our customers?
2. Do we know anything about it?
3. Do we have any agency? Can we effect any change?
4. What are the potential impacts on our employees?
5. What are the potential impacts on our reputation?

Wilson said the issue and decision in question—in this case, whether and how to speak out and act in response to the 2022 Supreme Court ruling to overturn *Roe v. Wade*—had to pass muster at each question.

Consider a different issue Wilson discussed with regard to whether Allstate should take a stance and lead from the front. He talked about climate change and the increasingly frequent wildfires that occur in California. He said the wildfire issue was "right up [their] alley" because it easily met the requirements of each of the five checkpoint questions. As an example, we have applied Wilson's framework to a scenario for illustration purposes only:

1. Will this help us do a better job for our customers?

Yes, this is major for our customers, as the wildfires are burning down our customers' houses. We can provide more insurance, if needed, to give them greater peace of mind and protect their families, loved ones, and assets against future fires, and we can issue checks for any damage assessed in current wildfires to help them restore their lives inasmuch as that is possible after such a devastating experience.

2. **Do we know anything about it?**

Yes, we know a lot about fires because we are in the risk-management and insurance business, and wildfires and other natural disasters are a running risk in our business.

3. **Do we have any agency? Can we effect any change?**

Yes, we know how to influence policy and get legislation passed in California, working with legislators and regulators to get stuff done.

4. **What are the potential impacts on our employees?**

Our employees like us taking the lead on the issue because it reflects well on the company.

5. **What are the potential impacts on our reputation?**

Taking the lead on this issue has either no effect or a positive effect on our reputation. There is little risk of it having a negative effect on our reputation.

Just as Wilson predicted, the wildfires were well within Allstate's value-based parameters as an issue it felt prepared to address. He said Allstate put 104 issues through its framework filters, ultimately concluding that if an issue is "related to climate change, privacy, or equity, call [Allstate]; that's where [the company] will lead." He went on to say that there were other issues that the company is not against but that did not pass through all its filters in its framework, and therefore it might support those issues in other ways but would not lead on them.

Returning his attention to the overturning of *Roe v. Wade*, Wilson said the decision about whether to take a stand did not feel as intuitive and was vetted through the same framework. The company decided that the issue did not affect its customers with relevance to its business because Allstate does not sell health insurance, so it was rerouted on the very first filter. Allstate decided to address it as an employee issue and respond to it as a healthcare matter its plan has always covered for its workforce. He said the company chose not to lead on that issue because "if businesses try to lead on everything, then they are going to lead on nothing." He ended that part of the discussion noting that it was important for Allstate to have developed a process to make values-driven, clear, and transparent decisions and to let everyone know about the process.

Dr. Martin Luther King Jr. said, "The time is always right to do what is right." Indeed, it is, and most management teams we have worked with want to do the right things, but sometimes what is right is not obvious.

A lot of managers find themselves in this predicament today when trying to make good decisions for their team or in response to individual requests from employees who report to them. The usual managerial decision pitfalls like perceptions of favoritism, bias, discrimination, or general unfairness seem riskier and more amplified in this business climate where people are more demanding, expectant, and sensitive and in environments where they can secretly record, quickly post updates on social media, or share only half the story or tell parts of it without context.

Doing what is right is also not as simple as making the same decision for every similar or identical request when they come from different people because employees are dealing with a variety of circumstances, strengths, weaknesses, and perceived or actual barriers. This is one of the many complexities of managing and leading people in corporations and organizations today.

To make the best decisions for and in response to your team, there are two key foundational steps to take. First, decide on a core set of values that your team will know, understand, and abide by, and, second, put those values into a decision-scoring mechanism that will help you *objectively* and *subjectively* evaluate the various factors that are going into any given decision. In business, people prefer black-and-white, efficient, data-driven, objective decisions. That is not always possible or realistic for managerial decisions regarding employees. There is a subjective element to these decisions. That's why (as we've outlined in past chapters) managers today need a high degree of emotional intelligence and maturity, a good dose of empathy, excellent communication skills, and the ability to think critically and quickly about decisions. Now, making those quick decisions oftentimes comes down to good judgment. There often are no objectively right or wrong answers, as many decisions can be argued either way, but strong managers need to be able to clearly articulate their decision and the reason for it, and it should be a sensible decision to any other reasonable business leader—even if they might have made a different decision.

Having clearly defined values in advance and a values-driven decision scoring system will be helpful assets when and if you ever need to explain and justify a decision in a compelling and convincing way—which is another key skill in decision-making. This should work, if not 100 percent of the time, almost all the time because, as you are using these tools, if a decisional direction you are considering is weak or middling, your tools should make that clear during your process and allow you to change course or strengthen your argument, evidence, and position.

The people asking about your decisions may not be in executive management; it could be someone on your team or your entire team. This is especially true if people talk and realize that on a similar issue, or what they perceive to be a similar issue, you decided in one direction for one team member and a different direction for another team member. Again, this does not mean your decision was wrong—there is some subjectivity and discretion in managerial decision-making. The key to protecting workplace culture when these questions arise is to be sincere and transparent about your thought process and to get ahead of assumptions.

Creating Your Decision Framework

While the Allstate example showcases decision-making for an entire enterprise involving multiple stakeholders, the process that company follows is the same one you can use to help you make decisions at a team or business-unit level and for individual employees. In these scenarios, it is key to articulate your values as a leader and define the values of the team. Thereafter, you can take a qualitative approach like Wilson did with Allstate and run decisions through several questions that move you closer to a clearer decision. Or you can combine the questions with numerical values to create a quantitative approach.

It can be helpful to develop a culture issues scorecard to make decisions that a company knows or believes will have a material impact on culture. You could develop something like this by talking with your team and incorporating their feedback into the scorecard you ultimately create. This type of tool helps individuals and teams uncover personal leadership values and mine for collective values to find harmony or address potential conflicts. As the leader, you ultimately decide on the final set of values for the team after you have accounted for and included the team's varying perspectives.

Also, remember that this process is a formulaic approach to help you get sharper at making decisions for your team when there may be competing priorities, differences in the needs and best fit for people even among similar requests, and other complexities that you need to sort through. You'll find over time that you'll intuitively know, like Wilson did about leading in response to the wildfires, which decision you should make. When you grow to that point, you may never or only occasionally need the decision-making framework or scoring system. For now, it is a good way to approach decisions as you learn the new workplace culture context and, specifically, what it means at your company and with your employees.

10

Responsibly Representing Others

O ne of the most relatable domains of public life we can turn to for insight on responsibly representing others is political leadership. The US political system is built on the trustee system of representation rather than the delegate system. A delegate representative merely goes into places and spaces and repeats exactly what their constituents have conveyed as their wishes, whereas a trustee representative is appointed or elected by their constituents to represent their perspective and adapt and make decisions as needed on their behalf and in their best interest based on the trustee's understanding of the outcomes, and the means to those outcomes, that the constituents prefer.

As a manager within your organization who is leading and representing people and working to build or enhance a purposeful culture, you are acting as a trustee. There are four key actions for you to take to represent your team responsibly and well.

Understand What's Most Important to Each Team Member

As a trustee representative, you may be speaking for your team as a whole or for an individual team member in rooms that they will never get to enter. If you are asked a question about a decision that could impact your team, knowing them well as a result of your many conversations will help you make a decision that they would be comfortable with.

For example, in addition to writing this book, we have been working together for almost six years. We know enough about each other's personalities, preferences, opinions, anxieties, likes, and dislikes that if one of us is absent and we have to decide on something as simple as the tone of a communication up to something as meaningful as the fee we would be willing to accept for a client engagement, either one of us could represent the pair and make a decision. Ninety-nine times out of a hundred, the decision is exactly what the absent person would have decided. This is the level to which you want to learn and understand what is important to your team so that you can represent them responsibly when they either cannot be or simply are not present to represent themselves.

Align on Team Values

We've already discussed at length the power of having shared values in the workplace, but the same benefits are seen at the team level. The same values that are part of a decision architecture (see the previous chapter) are also an important asset to navigate decisions as a trustee representative for your team.

With clarity on the beliefs and principles that you and your team hold in highest esteem, you are equipped to think through various scenarios in their absence and to consider what each person would want, what the team would want, and ultimately what would be best. Discussing this in advance positions you to be a strong and decisive representative for your team. This has implications for budget resources, development opportunities, and new projects that can raise the visibility of your team and their work.

Accept and Account for Your Limitations

While you may have done all the work to understand your colleagues both as individuals and as a collective team, there are factors that can limit your ability to represent someone on your team as well and as accurately as they deserve simply because you are not in a position to relate to them, such as in matters connected to identity or differences in skill sets.

For instance, it is common today for multidisciplinary teams to work together. With all the different skill sets on any given team, it is likely that the project leads or representatives attending meetings will need to speak for the entire team, including teammates whose skills are very different from the representative's own. If there are creative, financial, strategy, IT, and HR team members but only strategy leads in the room, the best approach would be to ask for time to report back with answers to questions about the cost and deadlines of the creative elements of the project. If the strategists speak extemporaneously without knowing at an instinctual level what is important to their creative colleagues and what the creatives most value, they might represent them from a place of limitation, which could result in an unideal outcome.

Whether you are representing your team in meetings about work products, social issues, organizational culture, or any other matter, make sure you know your team's general mindset and perspective as well as your limitations so that representation does not turn into misrepresentation.

Build Your Belief

Representing your team throughout your organization may sometimes take the form of promoting or selling someone else's abilities. This could be when you are advocating for someone on your team to be promoted, supported with a budget for a project, or given a new plum opportunity. It helps you represent your team well in these cases the more you believe in them and in what you are saying to influence others on their behalf.

People can sense intuitively both authenticity and insincerity, so build your belief in your team over time so that you can be a powerful and persuasive trustee on their behalf. We talk with our teams all the time about knowing and deliberately developing their numbers and their narrative. Their numbers are the performance data within our organization that tell a story about their productivity and profitability. Their narrative is the story that explains the impact of their work on client companies and the actions they have taken that resulted in their numbers. This combination makes sense at the company we work for because of the way our teams are set up and because thinking about one's performance in this way is part of our culture norms. Our colleagues who report directly to us may not always be working directly with us; they could be working on projects with other leaders all or most of any given year. Still, because we are responsible along with them for how they are positioned and promoted within the organization, we need their numbers and narrative to both build our belief and equip us to be effective representatives on their behalf.

Ask your employees to gather and share with you the most fitting information that helps you represent them well based on the culture at your company and the available data. This process puts you in a strong position to represent your team while modeling how they can step into the role of a trustee and responsibly represent others they will lead in the future.

11

The Art of Persuasion

It was the opening day of a continuing-education course. The promised curriculum was a three-day crash course on the art and science of negotiation. The first day started casually, with the professor walking around the classroom to introduce herself to students. People were eager to meet her. Oh, the stories she could tell—she had been involved in some of most notable negotiations of the recent past. The excitement students had for learning new skills seemed to be matched by the anticipation of hearing fascinating accounts of what it was like to sit at the negotiating table with world leaders. After brief introductions, she then turned the spotlight over to the students and asked each to speak briefly about why they had decided to pause their professional work for a few days and decamp to this lecture hall to improve their negotiation skills (after all, in this continuing-education program, students were typically mid-career).

One by one, the students shared what had brought them to the lecture hall; there were many lawyers whose firms regularly sent emerging leaders to this course, a few people in commercial real estate, one independent real-estate agent, and those from a smattering of other professions that require dealmaking as part of the job. Then, there was also someone who described her work as being a "general people manager." The professor furrowed her brow as this person shared her background. She then followed with, "What negotiations do *you* have to do?"—the general curiosity (or was it outright confusion?) evident in her voice. The way the student tells the story, she was completely caught off guard by the professor's question because her day-to-day experience was chock-full of negotiations. Sure, she wasn't spending weeks ticking through the terms of a complex multinational merger in a formal conference room, flanked by an army of fellow lawyers. However, from morning until night, she was trying to negotiate with her internal colleagues on a bevy of topics. She had carved out time from her busy professional life to double down on her negotiation skills because this was the primary capability she needed in order to be successful at work, so why was she getting confused looks on day one from the professor?

We open with this story because the ability to negotiate is not just for those who are formal dealmakers—there are many routine negotiations in a typical day's work at the office. And we balk at the notion that general managers might not need these skills; it is the informal interactions that dot the typical day at the office that sometimes can be the hardest to manage, and we applaud the woman who attended that continuing-education course, eager to apply proven negotiation tactics to her people-management challenges. But, relatedly, in the office there are perhaps even more moments of *persuasion*, which is a complementary skill to but also distinct from negotiation.

Adam Ferree, who lists his current role as the senior director of negotiation strategy and strategic partnerships at Walmart, published an article on LinkedIn parsing apart the two skills. In it, he writes, "Negotiation relies on two sides reaching a compromise. Persuasion is focused on convincing the opposing party to do what you want."[1] He goes on to emphasize that most negotiations involve a high degree of persuasion, so the skills continue to be used together.

When considering which skill—negotiation or persuasion—is most essential to managing the evolved expectations of workplace culture, we settle on persuasion because this work does include a high degree of convincing others to take an action or adopt a mindset that may be new; however, much of this work can veer into a negotiation quickly (so take that negotiation class, too!).

How to Persuade

There is a lot of convincing involved in building and maintaining an effective culture at work. Imagine you are trying to persuade other people to adopt a plan you feel is essential for your culture—be it to talk about an issue at work, elect not to talk about an issue at work, offer additional mental-health support for a colleague, or determine that enough support has been put in place to support teams. Any of these situations involves a calculated influence strategy.

Robert Cialdini is widely heralded as the expert on persuasion and influence in the workplace. His many books have sold more than seven million copies, and his research accomplishments in behavioral science were celebrated when he was elected to the American Academy of Arts and Sciences in 2018 and the National Academy of Sciences in 2019. In culling through his many opinions on how to persuade, one takeaway comes to the top, perhaps best summarized by best-selling author, podcast host, and NYU Stern School of Business professor of marketing Scott Galloway, who interviewed Cialdini. In response to one of Cialdini's key points on persuasion, Galloway remarked, "It's hard not to like people who like you."[2]

Liking is one of Cialdini's seven principles of persuasion (the others being reciprocity, scarcity, authority, consistency, social proof, and unity). Liking stands out in the context of the new expectations of workplace culture because in a world as polarized as ours, it seems that we are always on guard, ready to have a serious conversation or offer feedback to someone on how they could have better navigated a sticky situation.

However, while we are all on a journey of continuous improvement, Cialdini contends that liking is a critical component of doing good work in business. He notes that being likeable and liking others creates a feeling for both parties that makes them want to do work together, even bluntly noting in his book *Influence, New and Expanded: The Psychology of Persuasion* that "people prefer to say yes to individuals they like."[3] So how do you make yourself more likeable so that, when you need to persuade, you can guide the conversation to the outcome you desire?

Cialdini's research finds that many factors can communicate likeability (we recommend you pick up one of his books, which detail ample compelling research), but one tactic he encourages is to increase compliments, and we would likewise encourage managers to try this. Cialdini's research suggests that when people offer compliments, they become more liked. At work, we typically get to know those in our teams or extended teams; this is not an environment of absolute strangers. And while large companies can have tens or hundreds of thousands of people, you typically do start to develop a circle of contacts in your workplace network. These are the people who likely make up the community with which you will be managing workplace culture issues, and these people may be those with whom you need to use your skills of persuasion. So, within that group, it is wise to be liked, and that's where committing to routinely delivering compliments can help soften the ground.

Cialdini found that he was thinking complimentary things but not saying them (which, if compliments are a currency in the persuasion game, meant he was practically throwing away money). So he trained himself on a very practical skill because it primed the ground for effective persuasive interactions. He explains in the podcast with Galloway and reiterates in his book, "When I hear myself saying something complimentary about a person to myself, I move it from my mind to my tongue."

The next time you hear someone say something that you find to be particularly insightful, tell them so; when someone excels in a meeting, jot down a short note of praise; when someone gives a skillful response to a tough client question, say that you wrote it down because you loved that phrasing. Doing these types of things makes you more likeable so that when you approach a situation where you need to exert persuasion and influence—on a topic of workplace culture—you will be in a stronger position to do so.

But if you've done the likeability work and you're now actually in the throes of persuading, we find the following two things work particularly well and should be part of any persuasive conversation on culture:

- *Anchor any culture-based request, plan, or strategy back to the business data:* We mentioned in chapter two some of the strong financial returns that companies with strong cultures have seen, so remind people that what you're advocating for can bolster business results. We've all seen the statistics on how people need things repeated several times for a concept to sink in, and the same goes here. Repeat those business statistics again and again.

- *Point out how this action advances the stated values or mission of the company:* If you have stated tenets of your workplace culture—and we've found that most companies do—use them in your argument. This can be as straightforward as saying, "Our company says it stands for [insert value], and this is a demonstration of that work in action." It's hard for someone to argue with doing something you consider "innovative" if "We are innovative" is on a poster in the break room. Now, of course, different people can interpret values differently, but even with subjectivity in mind, we've found that this is a simple but very effective approach.

How Managers and Teams Can Avoid Persuasion Pitfalls

Cialdini's conversation with Galloway includes particularly insightful comments on the mindset with which you should approach persuasion; Cialdini reminds us to "give grace."

Many of the interviews we conducted with business leaders that informed the research for this book reinforce this advice—in our hyperpolarized world, people are craving a work environment where compromise is a valued outcome. As a human-resources professional at a multinational company mentioned to us, "Compromise is a leadership skill. The more we are all trying to get our own way, we aren't going to win. There really is no winning if we cannot focus on what we can do to move forward productively." That brings us to a pitfall that can doom a persuasive argument: refusing to negotiate. You can be persuasive, but keep in mind that some of the expectations of new employees can feel like radical changes from the way things have always been, and businesses can balk at change that happens too abruptly. If, instead, a compromised plan is needed to demonstrate some progress, some is better than none when it comes to many of the issues pertaining to workplace culture. Take, for example, a culture that says one of its values is employee wellness, but the workload at this company is newly relentless because demand for the company's services has skyrocketed. Because of this surge in demand (a key tenet of the company's business strategy), company leaders celebrate how strong the financial projections are for the year. Employees grow frustrated that, to meet the demand, they must compromise their wellness. Perhaps the dominant employee sentiment becomes

"We need to stop talking about how in demand our services are because it runs counter to our value of wellness." However, because this growth is key to the business strategy, leaders have no plans to turn away work. What might a compromise entail?

A team could work to build a culture where managers try to identify work that is particularly interesting to their employees—things that align with their growth goals, interests, or beliefs. Now, sure, some work just needs to get done, so not all projects on an employee's docket will stir them personally, but looking for opportunities that do could become an expectation. This approach would support the business model, but it also could help reinforce a culture where employees feel the company respects their wellness—in this particular instance, employees might feel healthier working on projects of personal interest.

So, as you set out to flex your skills of persuasion, resist the pitfall of avoiding compromise. It does not signal weakness in many cases. Instead, it can be essential to progress.

Top Takeaway on Persuasion

If you take one thing away from this chapter, we hope it's to approach the work of persuasion less as a battle to be fought and more as a quest to be a good partner to those around you. We've found that you get more culture work done if you're coming at it from a positive posture and not a hard-charging "this must be done now, or else" approach. Persuading others to adopt your plans, particularly around culture-building work, can seem scary to many, so communicating that you're a reasonable—and likeable—colleague sets you up for the best outcomes.

12

How to Forgive

With various generations, identities, and beliefs combining in today's workplace, forgiveness is an essential skill. Everyone should learn it, embrace it, and live it daily—and people managers should lead the way.

What is forgiveness? We define it quite simply as the act of letting go of ill feelings toward someone else. It is both emotional and behavioral. When you forgive, you make a mental shift. After you switch how you are thinking about a moment or person that offended you, noticeable behavioral changes follow. Mentally, either you decide to forget what happened, like in the case of Pastor James—an exemplary community leader whom you'll meet later in chapter thirteen—or you decide the offense is no longer relevant and worth your attention. Once you forget the event or reposition it as irrelevant in your mind, your actions naturally change toward whomever or whatever upset you. Prior to forgiving, you might avoid the offender(s) or interact with them with contention and distrust; after forgiving, you go back to harmonious or neutral interactions where there is no tension. The energy between two people or groups before and after forgiveness is palpable.

Let's consider a more formal definition of forgiveness. Psychological-science researchers at the Greater Good Science Center at the University of California, Berkeley, describe it as "a conscious, deliberate decision to release feelings of resentment or vengeance toward a person or group who [you feel] has harmed you, regardless of whether they actually deserve your forgiveness."[1] The last part of this formal definition—*whether they actually deserve your forgiveness*—is key.

Often, our perception is that our reputation and self-respect are at stake if we forgive someone who has said or done something wrong to us. Our ego and pride, and norms of business— such as the will to win—can tell us that we must stand up for ourselves by holding on to the offense. Our predisposition for fairness and desire to be right can get in the way of us simply being able to say to ourselves, "I know they didn't mean it" or "I choose to believe they didn't mean it. I will forget the offense and move on." Note that forgiving does not mean condoning. You can acknowledge that something was wrong while forgiving the wrong that was done. For this reason, forgiveness requires a higher level of awareness, maturity, and self-confidence than do some of the other workplace culture skills required in this modern context. However, forgiving, as difficult as it may be, can be learned with effort and persistence.

Before we move further into a discussion of forgiveness and exactly how to practice it, it is also worth noting what *unforgiveness* is and why it can be so stifling for colleagues and teams at work. Kizito D. Kalima, founder of the Peace Center for Forgiveness and Reconciliation, knows a lot about unforgiveness. He survived genocide in his home country, Rwanda. His organization's website states that he was once consumed with destructive anger about what happened to him before eventually experiencing transformational healing. Kalima says, "To forgive is to set a prisoner free and discover the prisoner was you."

A popular quote says, "Holding on to anger is like grasping a hot coal with the intent of throwing it at someone else; you are the one who gets burned." Such aphorisms generate powerful mental pictures of the unhelpful, unproductive, and quite harmful effects unforgiveness can have among people or groups. Imagine this sentiment amplified across a team, business unit, or organization. In fact, we can see clearly what this looks like in real life by looking at the geopolitical climate globally. Political violence, war, and unrest are literally compounded manifestations of unforgiveness between people, groups, or countries.

Warring in the workplace is also destructive. In research with two hundred office workers in Washington, DC, and manufacturing employees in the Midwest, psychologists who study the science of forgiveness found that harboring resentment against coworkers is linked to negative health and business outcomes.[2] That is, unforgiveness can lead to higher rates of call-offs; increased anxiety and other emotional pain; physical discomfort such as headaches; poor or unrealized project outcomes; and even such severe impacts as verbal abuse, aggressive or violent behavior, resignations, and revenue losses.

Organizations with people managers who model and teach their teams how to forgive can reap benefits in the form of a more engaging, peaceful workplace culture and greater employee and revenue retention.

How to Actually Forgive

Dr. Everett L. Worthington Jr., a clinical psychologist and professor emeritus at Virginia Commonwealth University, studies virtuous behaviors such as hope and forgiveness.[3] His research insights have been cited almost 43,000 times. He created the REACH Forgiveness model, which offers a formulaic and measurable approach to the act of forgiving. The acronym stands for:

> Recall the hurt
> Empathize with the other person
> Altruism is a gift
> Commit to forgiveness
> Hold on to forgiveness

> Here's how we apply it:

R—Recall the Hurt

Take time to reflect on exactly what hurt and offended you. Articulate to yourself why you were upset or wounded by what happened. Taking time to process this is not only healing in and of itself; it also helps you clearly identify which of your values you feel was violated by the other person. This can be helpful for you and the other person for a couple reasons. One, it helps you remember that your values are yours and that not everyone has the same values. So maybe what happened to you could be considered objectively wrong—meaning many or most people would agree that it was wrong. Or, perhaps, it felt wrong to you because of an expectation you hold within yourself as a result of your past experiences. Regardless of which reason applies, remember the earlier formal definition of forgiveness and the fact that it requires letting go, whether you believe the other person deserves it or not. The forgiveness is really for you. The second reason introspection is helpful is it allows you to be very clear with the other person about what caused you harm. This specificity gives them the opportunity to choose to not repeat the harm in the future. To avoid creating more hurt during the process of forgiveness, when you share with the other person what bothered you, phrase it in the first person. Instead of "You made me angry or hurt me . . . ," say, "I was angry or hurt because . . ."

E—Empathize with the Other Person

After completing the first step, especially when you consider differences in values, it becomes easier to see why the other person may have done or said whatever offended you. Again, this does not necessarily mean you are condoning it, but at least you can hopefully better understand it. To complete this step, you can do a thought experiment: think on your own about what you know of the person and mentally build an argument in their defense. If you find it hard to do this, then it may be the perfect time to have a conversation with the other person to simply ask what led to what they said or did. Tone is important in this conversation. This should not come across as an accusatory question but as a humble inquiry. For example, instead of asking "Why would you say or do that?" you can say, "I would really like to understand more about how you see this. What led to what was said?"

A—Altruism Is a Gift

Think about a time when you made a mistake and someone forgave you, even if you have to go back to childhood when a parent or other family member, teacher, or classmate forgave you. Remember how badly you felt for what you did or said and how relieved you felt when you realized you had been forgiven. Embrace the opportunity to give this gift to your coworker by leaning into forgiveness. The faster you do this, and the more often you do this, the easier and more natural it becomes.

C—Commit to Forgiveness

Depending on the depth of the offense, you may feel anger or unforgiveness trying to resurface even as you're taking the steps to forgive. While this is frustrating, it is a great opportunity to further practice forgiveness because the recurring negative emotions signal that you may have repressed your feelings about what happened rather than completely faced and dismissed them. This is the mental equivalent of throwing everything on your desk or in your bedroom into a drawer or closet instead of taking the time to sort through your things, clean up, and discard what is no longer useful or needed. If you feel negative emotions coming back up again, go back to step one. Don't simply throw your emotions in a mental drawer or closet. Instead, recall and reflect on the hurt again, go through the process of empathizing again, and commit once more to forgiveness. Repeating the process for a second or third time is okay. As an additional step, talking to a neutral manager, leader, or an HR business partner—or even calling an employee assistance program hotline, if that benefit is provided by your workplace, where someone can listen and help you process the remaining feelings—can help you finish the process of forgiving.

H—Hold On to Forgiveness

Remember that if you find this whole process challenging, time consuming, or annoying, the benefits are real. By practicing forgiveness, you will feel better and perform better at work, and so will your team. Have you ever walked into a room where there are two people who do not like each other? You can feel the tension. That is such an uncomfortable feeling for those involved as well as for uninvolved team members. You will have a better daily experience in the workplace, whether virtually or in person, where you spend one third or more of your life, by learning and practicing the skill of forgiveness. It is worth the time. Finally, concentrate on the fact that the more you forgive, the easier it is to forgive, and you are likely to see spillover effects in other parts of your life. With the new purpose of workplace culture being to build better workplaces, better people, and a better world, that is a benefit in itself.

Plot Twist: Self-Forgiveness Is a Necessary Skill, Too

As we consider the importance of forgiveness in the workplace, the focus tends to be on others. But self-forgiveness can be an important act as well. Many types of conflicts can happen in the workplace, stemming from a span of differences ranging from different management styles to different identities.

Depending on what happens during the conflict, two or more people may not only be holding a grudge against each other; they may also be feeling shame within themselves. This can be especially true for sensitive topics such as racism or sexism where certain racial and ethnic groups or genders already are prone to generalized shame because of judgment rooted in historical bias and conflict.

Shame and self-unforgiveness can also be particularly acute for someone who has spoken or acted quite harshly or dramatically toward a coworker and later felt embarrassed for their lack of professionalism and loss of self-control.

Self-unforgiveness is just as harmful as not forgiving someone else because it results in unproductive and damaging rumination where you keep replaying the scenario in your head, thinking about what you could have said or done differently. This takes away from the mental energy and resources you could be using toward good work. It also creates differences in your behavior that may disrupt collaboration and teamwork.

In cases where we need to let go of shame and engage in self-compassion, Dr. Worthington Jr., the forgiveness psychologist, also offers a helpful evidence-based practice that can guide you back to a centered and productive place. We'll call this approach the "Six Rs of Self-Forgiveness":

- *Receive* general forgiveness—visualize yourself as forgiven and choose to believe that this is true outside of yourself.

- *Repair* relationships—apologize for what you said or did and do so without turning it into absolution, which is a need or expectation for your apology to be accepted. Acceptance is up to the other person, but genuinely apologizing helps begin your process to forgive yourself and heal. Additionally, if there are other steps you can take to make amends for what you did, this can be restorative as well. Do this from a place of understanding the impact of your actions, not from a place of shame.

- *Rethink* ruminations—perfectionism or a strong desire to undo the past can cause us to constantly think about what happened. Of course, this is futile. Think about a more productive and helpful idea you can focus on, and every time you find your mind wandering back into rumination, make the mental pivot to the more helpful thinking.

- *REACH* emotional self-forgiveness—follow for yourself the REACH model previously shared for use with others.

- *Rebuild* self-acceptance—sometimes we can be much harder on ourselves than on others, especially when we realize, *Ugh, I knew better.* Acknowledge that nearly everyone has had a lapse in judgment at some point in life, and remind yourself that it is okay and that you have taken proper action to make amends. If it helps, talk with someone else who will say this to you.

- *Resolve* to live virtuously—take the time to really understand why you said or did that for which you are now seeking self-forgiveness. The clearer you can be about what you did, why, how awful it feels, and why you never want to do it again, the likelier it is you will make a better choice in the future and not make the same mistake again.

How Managers and Teams Can Apply the Principles of Forgiveness

As a manager or team member, if you know there are tensions festering in your team, you can lead the colleagues involved back to a place of peace and productivity in a few ways:

- Cue a conversation around forgiveness and share some of the research data on what unforgiveness can do to individual health and team unity. Lead a group exercise where everyone shares something for which they have not forgiven someone else or themselves and articulates what was hurtful and why they want to forgive. This can be completed aloud, or people can write it out and never share it with anyone else. Decide which way to do the exercise based on the team's norms when it comes to emotional vulnerability. Either approach is beneficial because both actions—speaking aloud or writing it down—help people process and let go. Some of the prompts that can be used to complete this exercise are:
  - I felt hurt when . . .
  - I felt angry because . . .
  - I felt sad after . . .
  - This felt personal because . . .

- I really value [insert value], and that value was violated when . . .
- What happened struck a negative chord because . . .
- What happened triggered me because it reminded me of the time . . .
- In the future, I would prefer it if . . .
- I do not condone what happened, but I can see how the person I want to forgive acted the way they did because . . .
- Evidence that what happened was not personal includes . . .
- If it were me, I would have handled the situation differently by . . .
- A great memory I have with the person I want to forgive is . . .
- A great quality I have noticed about the person I want to forgive is . . .
- I choose to forgive this person because . . .
- I have been feeling [insert emotion(s)] and experiencing [insert physical effects] since this situation happened, and I do not want to continue feeling this way—so I am letting it all go as of now.

- Turn an upcoming project into an opportunity to rebuild the team's bonds and trust by identifying a clear goal and giving each person a specific role in achieving that goal. Design the project in such a way that everyone depends on each other to be successful. Ideally, this would come after a thoughtful, well-managed conversation about the issue that created unforgiveness. The project then becomes a real and symbolic act of reconciliation and reunification.

- Sometimes the process of forgiveness reveals that the best way to avoid further and future offense is to mutually agree to not work closely together anymore or to move on in peace. In cases such as these, managers can facilitate an employee voluntarily transferring to a new location or business unit. This step should be taken only after completing the REACH Forgiveness model so that those involved do not take any "prisoners" or "hot coals" with them as they move on.

Learning from Leaders in Action

13

Who Was Taught to Do This?
The Consummate Community Leaders

By this point in the book, you are likely well versed in our thesis:

- Today's employees have new expectations as they view the workplace as the "town square" instead of as a place to only work.
- Traditional management education doesn't include the skills needed to lead effectively amid these new expectations.
- The new skills needed include conversing, listening, empathizing, deciding, representing, persuading, and forgiving.

- Practically every role requires these skills, as all job types have a role to play in building a culture that meets the evolved expectations of today's workforce.

Now, while many in corporate America or business-school settings are scrambling to learn this new management skill set, our research finds that some professional tracks have curricula on how to teach and lead in this way. Faith-based practitioners and some nonprofit leaders are trained in some of these precise capabilities.

When learning something new, it's always helpful to have an image of what excellence looks like, and for that, we turn to remarks from several interviews we conducted as part of the research for this book. During each interview, we asked the person to speak with great specificity about how they learned—are learning—and/ or implement each of the seven skills at work. Included below, and in the subsequent chapter, we outline their top tips and tricks.

In this chapter, we speak to two people who are "best practice" models. We highlight them because they are in fields that in some cases include education on how to do this work well. First names have been changed.

• • •

Pastor James is the founder of a community-based nonprofit and the pastor of a local church. He is warm and determined and a relentless fundraiser and advocate who can effectively build coalitions across government offices, community leaders, religious organizations, and businesses. His leadership is deeply faith based—often quoting Scripture—and he complements his religious focus with keen business skills and savvy networking. His Rolodex of well-connected local leaders is impressive, and he knows how to turn his inspiring words into concrete actions that benefit his neighborhood and the broader city where he lives and works.

As we continue our investigation of the new skills that business leaders need, Pastor James is a stellar example of someone who has already mastered these capabilities—his pastoral education included coursework on how to learn such. Take it from the expert:

Pastor James on the Skill of Conversing

"I learned this from 'forced' interactions with people with whom I was uncomfortable."

Pastor James shared stories about his childhood, including several about one of his teachers. This teacher was always introducing Pastor James, then a young boy, to family and friends. In any one of these situations, young Pastor James had to come up with something to say to these people. He credits these discussions with strangers as teaching him how to strike up a conversation with someone who comes from a different neighborhood, has different beliefs, or is of an entirely different age or political orientation. He said he then refined that same skill while in seminary, where he was one of only a few Black students in a predominantly conservative white community. He went so far as to say that he was in a setting of "forced" conversation but one that he considers a forma-tive life experience that is the basis of his success.

KEY TAKEAWAY Welcome "forced" interactions; from challeng-ing yourself to talk to your Uber driver, to introducing yourself to the new colleague at work, to ditching your favorite person at the team happy hour and going to meet someone new—change your mindset from *This is worthless schmoozing and small talk* to *I am working on a skill that's needed for my career.*

Pastor James on the Skill of Listening

> *"You can't make a good argument if you haven't lis-tened to the other side."*

Business leaders oftentimes self-identify as being in some way competitive. Sure, our own style of competition may vary, but there is often some inherent competitiveness among colleagues. Pastor James said that he is deeply competitive, and he is reminded of that most when he's listening. Yes, he wants to win most arguments that he enters, and, he said, the only way to do so is to listen to the other side—that's how you know what to say and when. Pastor James reminds himself that listening is not just about what you're *not* doing (talking), but it's about what you *are* doing. And for him, it's that he *gets* information.

KEY TAKEAWAY Listening is not a passive activity. It's some-thing that gives you a lot, much of which can increase your com-petitive posture.

Pastor James on the Skill of Decision-Making

"I make decisions that are thoroughly thought-out. I have little tricks I use . . . I wait twenty-four hours before acting on something."

Pastor James said it's a complete red flag if someone is rushing him, and he flat out refuses to make a decision if he hasn't heard both well-researched sides of an argument. This is his analytical, methodical approach, but he's also candid that he weighs the data with his intuition. Now, we know that many a corporate leader would pounce on someone if they said, "I'm making this decision based on my intuition," but that's actually not what Pastor James is suggesting when he talks about using his intuition. Instead, he mixes intuition with data and, most of all, with time. He's found twenty-four hours works for him; perhaps you have a different time stamp, but the bottom line is that it's key to have a set amount of time. We know the working world can sometimes prize speed and immediate gratification, but Pastor James doesn't cave to that pressure.

KEY TAKEAWAY Require counterpoints and deflect the impulse to rush into something. Determine a set amount of time before your decision will be made.

Pastor James on the Skill of Representing Others

"While you might be the one talking, quote other people to make your point."

Pastor James learned to speak on behalf of others by leading youth groups, a fraternity in college, and the Black student union. He's most effective when he resists the urge to paraphrase, and instead he uses the precise words and phrases of those whom he is representing. So, jot down an actual quote of something someone said—there is true power in a person's original words. He also said that any time he's representing a group with a specific interest, he not only goes in with a tight argument representing the group's position but also reminds himself about what unifies us all. In the case of his community-based work in the United States, he says he keeps this in mind: we are all Americans—whether Black, white, rich, poor, educated, uneducated—we all want the American Dream. So next time you're heading into that contentious meeting, try to ground yourself by recognizing one thing that unites everyone in attendance.

KEY TAKEAWAY Humanize, humanize, humanize. Speak about people using their own words and remind yourself that you have things in common with those on the "other side."

Pastor James on Persuasion

"Work 1:1 or in large groups."

Pastor James knows that he's most effective in convincing someone of a position when he's in the intimate setting of a 1:1 conversation. He also spoke about how a large group can be particularly effective to make a strong, inspiring case, too. This leaves us with the conclusion to avoid middle-sized groups. Here's our hypothesis as to why: In a 1:1 setting, you can address challenges or skepticism directly, and in a large group, individuals can be influenced by the energy of the crowd. However, a middle-sized setting can be small enough that dissenters feel emboldened to challenge you publicly, which can cause factions to form within the group.

KEY TAKEAWAY Think about environmental cues when assembling programs or conversations, and consider what size and scale is best for the opportunity.

Pastor James on Forgiveness

*"Walking around angry at someone is like drinking poison and waiting for the other person to die."** *

Pastor James was firm on the topic of forgiveness; the key, he said, is to forget. He said that he's blessed to have the ability to simply not remember. Of course, this requires immense discipline and a healthy sense of humor, but he said this is core to survival. He is proud that he flat out doesn't remember certain things that could cause him to feel pain, hurt, or resentment in the long term. At work, we can assume that this, too, will require people to move on as we all stumble with managing the evolved expectations of employees and, at the same time, cancel culture. When decisions or positions are made swiftly and have enduring reputational impacts, how do

---

* This saying and similar ones have also been attributed to many past leaders, including Saint Augustine and Nelson Mandela.

we teach each other to forget? Pastor James implores us, as he implores his parishioners, to block it out.

KEY TAKEAWAY The adage "Good athletes have short memories" should become "Good employees have short memories"—or, put more colloquially, "Move on."

• • •

In complement to Pastor James, please meet Luisa, who has worked in and led nonprofit organizations, including in an executive-level role with direct responsibility for board leadership and fundraising as well as overseeing operations, programming, growth, and community relations.

Luisa is measured and always prepared for her responsibilities. She takes careful notes, asks for time to reflect, and then is clear in her recommended path forward. She is also warm, laughing easily and asking questions that make those around her want to weigh in. When talking to Luisa, it's clear she is listening; her focused gaze seems to block out distractions, and she makes you feel like you're the only person in the world.

Luisa is also deeply self-reflective; she candidly pointed out to us that while she's been exceedingly successful in her professional career, she's not "good in the moment." Instead, she is confident in her need to process information before acting. Part of this processing takes place during her daily runs—a ritual that helps her work through her thinking, prepare for what's next, and consider how she might manage a certain situation. This methodical self-awareness is a hallmark of Luisa's leadership style, from which we can all learn a great deal.

Luisa on the Skill of Conversing

"I specifically plan for how I'm going to go in the room; humor or a good question can acknowledge why we're here or deescalate if the mood is tense. This gets things going."

Luisa is fascinated with how people learn, so she doesn't come off as nervous about the lack of control that defines many conversations—after all, nothing kills a dialogue like someone who feels on-script. However, Luisa advocates for planning the first *moments* of a conversation. She mentions that this might involve writing down her key points and approaching how she'll "enter" the conversation with a plan. Once she's past the introductory moments, she resists the impulse to over-index on providing information and instead moves into the posture of a facilitator— encouraging people to talk and deriving meaning from their contributions. However, if the conversation gets into a territory where she is put on the spot, she might resist responding in the moment and instead try to redirect and ask questions of others—a way to "gather information" that she can mull over post-conversation.

KEY TAKEAWAY There is a significant difference between orchestrating a conversation and scripting one. Orchestration focuses on having some select organizational principles to get yourself in the room, set the tone, and collect information. It doesn't feel stiff, but it's not the Wild West, either.

Luisa on the Skill of Listening

"I look for what the person is saying that they aren't really saying. It's not always the words coming out of their mouth that are most important. Instead, I focus on the intention of what they're saying."

Luisa appears to approach listening a bit like a radiologist running an X-ray. She tries to get through the initial layers (the words) and instead look at the skeleton of the conversation (the intention). In a world focused on speed, with thousands of emails and fast-turn text exchanges shot out to our contacts daily, we've become reliant on getting words out fast. Take the autocomplete function on our phones—it literally completes our sentences at a speed faster than we can type. However, Luisa has the discipline to look past the words and think something to the effect of, *I know you're saying _____, but I'm hearing _____.* To do this, Luisa must rely on all the context around the actual words: the body language, the time of day, the setting, the relationship, the mood, the level of trust—the list of nonverbal signals could go on and on. All of those factors are inputs into the intention for which Luisa is listening.

KEY TAKEAWAY It may feel customary to home in on words. How many of us have doggedly tried to win an argument with the line "But you *said* [fill in the blank]"? Consider how to weigh the words as one input but not as the only one. And, as you listen and form a hypothesis of what the intention behind the words might be, test it. While listening, chime in with "I think I'm hearing you say _____; is that correct?"

Luisa on Decision-Making

"This is not traditional decision-making; this is about weighing diverse factors and moving forward."

Luisa contrasted her style to traditional decision-making, so let's first start by considering a definition of "traditional" decision-making. Perhaps the most typical and structured form is exemplified by the established "decision tree" tool. *Harvard Business Review*'s 1964 piece "Decision Trees for Decision Makers" is still prominently featured in the journal's suggested readings for decision-making. The author clearly defines the highly structured way that decision trees can affect work, and an overview of the article notes that the tool "helps business managers resolve uncertainties . . . It clarifies the choices, risks, objectives, monetary gains, and information needs involved. Whether simple or complex in layout, the decision tree always combines action choices with different possible events or the results of action affected by uncontrolled circumstances."[1] But this is quite different from how Luisa explained her process; instead of choosing a course of action, Luisa spoke about *making progress* (and perhaps was implying that the diverse factors that make up a decision when it comes to managing conversations of societal significance render the decision less about *deciding* on something and more about moving forward a bit). Yes, certainly progress of any kind is a decision of sorts, but the verbiage of progress implies that the issue will remain after the decision is made. We will likely make progress for today but not close the issue. Instead, we'll need to revisit it tomorrow, and again, and again. That's likely a needed mindset shift for today's managers—moving from making a decision to "close" an issue to making progress that's sufficient for today.

KEY TAKEAWAY This work will not end. Just as chronic conditions are never cured, the needs and preferences of today's employees will not be solved if we can just identify the "right" option on a real or metaphorical decision tree. Instead, consider decision-making a day-to-day practice.

Luisa on Representing Others

> *"I do not represent [someone's position] if I do not have a really clear understanding of their thinking."*

Luisa noted that her team sometimes must be thinking, *Why is she asking so many questions?* She acknowledged that, at her executive level, the assumption may likely be that she should just be interested in the surface of certain projects, but she was quick to reorient that logic to the task of representing others. Luisa believes that she absolutely cannot generalize when representing others. Instead, she emphasized, as a leader, she needs to be able to give examples. That requires a deep understanding of the person, program, topic, etc., at hand. And that's why she doggedly asks questions and is aware that it may come off as micromanagement. The distinction, it seems, is that she's not asking those questions because she wants to express an opinion on how to manage the situation; instead, she's asking questions so that she can answer future questions about how others are managing the situation. The nuance is an important one.

Luisa also noted that when it comes to representing others, she uses a skill from her formal training on issues of equity and racial justice. She advised, "Never speak as a 'we'; always speak from the position of 'I.'" That framing of never speaking as a "we" and instead speaking from an "I" has strong application in the workplace. For example, Luisa's tip would lead us to consider advising that a millennial manager avoid saying, "We millennials feel this way," and instead say, "From my perspective as a female millennial in the American Midwest, these are some of the trends and things I've seen." Therefore, encouraging leaders and managers to speak about the many ways that these new expectations are manifesting at work—based on what they are seeing individually—will be essential.

KEY TAKEAWAY Representing others means being equipped to do so, and being equipped means (1) having enough information, and (2) knowing the limitations of your information. Balance getting enough specifics with avoiding generalizations.

Luisa on the Skill of Persuasion

> *"I have to be careful that I don't start seeing too much of the other side of the argument and forget the ten things I have on my side of the argument."*

Luisa humbly admitted that while she's quite strong at conversing and listening, persuasion is where she wants to improve. To elevate her skills, she's learning from others—watching the tactics that those who are persuasive use day-to-day. As Luisa works to uplevel her persuasive skills, she focuses on a few questions. Ahead of a situation where she'll need to be persuasive, she considers:

- What would make this person say yes?
- What is the shared ground on which we can all stand?

She noted, however, that while she can be prepared with answers to those important questions, she can become distracted by the counterpoints that someone raises in the moment. All of a sudden, she then is laser focused on their points, and that's what can cause her to forget the compelling argument she prepared. She pointed to empathy here as a crutch: "I'm too empathetic," she mused. But she also noted that she tends to avoid conflict, which can be an element of a persuasive conversation. To manage her dislike for conflict, Luisa noted, the skill of reframing is helpful. If an exchange starts to feel combative, she views it as an opportunity for her to take back control of the conversation by reframing what they are there to accomplish; for that, it seems that the answer to one of her preparation questions, "What is the shared ground on which we can all stand?," is particularly helpful. Neutralizing a moment of tension by pointing out that both parties do have things in common can work well.

KEY TAKEAWAY Persuasion may be a skill that is best learned in the apprenticeship model: you find someone who does it well; you watch them, sit next to them in conversation, and note how they manage things; and then you try it yourself.

Luisa on the Skill of Forgiveness

"I don't like to hold grudges because they get in the way."

Luisa talked about forgiveness as if she were describing a powerful and productive tailwind—you can keep moving if you forgive. The alternative, which she described as a grudge, can be a disruptive headwind that makes work very hard. When she doesn't forgive, she assumes a very cautious posture, even withdrawing from work. She doesn't want to be in an environment where she withdraws from work, so she tries to forgive. She did note, however, that forgiving can require an exchange between parties. She spoke about forgiveness less as a personal, quiet exercise and more as a shared experience. She gave an example of how two people in conflict could agree to a conversation with specific guidelines:

- Person 1: State what you heard Person 2 say in a matter-of-fact way.
- Person 2: Correct what may have been a misconception or mishearing.
- *Swap roles and repeat.*

This "concrete process," as Luisa called it, can provide the infrastructure needed for the two parties to forgive.

KEY TAKEAWAY Sometimes forgiveness is not an organic process, one that might hinge on individual soul-searching to "get over it" or the power of time passing to blunt the initial hurt. Instead, consider if a formalized process may speed up or better facilitate forgiveness.

14

Who Is Learning to Do This?
The Consummate Business Leaders

As part of our journey to master the new skills required of today's managers, yes, it's critical to know what it looks like to master these skills, but it's equally helpful to hear about someone who is still in the process of learning to use these new skills. For that, we turn to Daniel and Karine. Both work in large, global corporate companies, and, similar to Pastor James and Luisa in the previous chapter, we interviewed Daniel and Karine as part of our research. We asked each to specifically talk about their experience learning the seven skills that we advocate for in this book. In contrast to Pastor James and Luisa—who work in religious and nonprofit roles and whose education included some guidance on how to adopt and implement these skills—Daniel and Karine work in the precise types of environments where in the not-so-distant past employees might have expected to actively avoid flexing some of these skills and instead spend their "at work" hours laser focused on work only. But now, these same environments are where Daniel and Karine have employees who expect to balance an intense focus on work with discussion and debate on issues of societal, political, and personal significance. That's why Daniel and Karine have had to adjust their management styles accordingly. These are profiles of precisely how they have learned—and are still learning—to do that. Their first names have been changed.

• • •

Daniel started his career in politics, and from there he moved into consulting, where he's held numerous roles and is now in a leadership position—a role that he described by saying, "Overseeing a large team means realizing that every few days, someone is having one of the most difficult or significant days of their life—a major surgery, the birth of a child, the death of a parent, the purchase of a home . . . I have to stay attuned to that."

Daniel is a no-nonsense type—he moves quickly, he shoots off emails at a rapid clip, and his language is direct. In a high-stakes situation, he can command a room of executives with his confident and fluid verbal delivery, perhaps leveraging his background in politics to influence even the most skeptical party. And clients love him not just because of his confidence in the room but also because he is endlessly responsive and a fount of wise and effective business counsel. Daniel responds to every email and always picks up his phone. He also is a data guy; he is always drawing on financial statistics about the impact of his team's work or what financial upside you can expect if you proceed with his preferred direction. Daniel's fast pace does not compromise his congeniality. Somehow, as he's whizzing through the office or jumping from Zoom meeting to Zoom meeting, he finds time to stop and ask you a thoughtful question that demonstrates he was completely listening to you the last time you spoke. But while Daniel can make you feel truly heard, don't for a second slouch on your work; Daniel is tough and has sky-high expectations of himself and others.

You may well know a Daniel type on your team. Highly successful, very busy, committed to excellence, competitive but caring. And Daniel—who emits confidence in the corporate environment— himself admitted that the past few years have required him to start learning new skills. In summarizing his journey, he said, referring to the COVID-19 pandemic and all that happened during that time, "I don't think many of us have gone through the last couple years and not been transformed by the experience." As Daniel reflected on how he's learned these seven new skills, he added an eighth— we can think of it as a bonus skill—and we start there.

Daniel on Managing the Role of Work in Life

"I changed from living to work to working to live. What I earn through work enables me to have the quality of life I want."

Daniel talked about who he is today by providing a counterpoint that he said encapsulates who he was pre-pandemic. He shared that during a particularly busy stint at work, he would drive in to the office most weekends. On his way out the door one Sunday morning, his child asked him why he had to go to work. To that, he responded, "Because my client needs me," to which his child mumbled, "I wish I were one of your clients." He clutched his heart when sharing that story.

Daniel believes that the pandemic offered him the opportunity to reshuffle how he serves his clients and, simultaneously, lives a fulfilling and present family life. Whereas pre-pandemic value might have been calculated by the amount of facetime with clients, now, he said, he can provide strong value and still command flexibility. Specifically, he said being home for dinner is a new and firm expectation he has of himself. To do this and make other work-life tweaks, he said he had to teach himself to be comfortable disappointing people at work. Notably, he pointed out that when he used to say "yes" to any ask, his behavior suggested that he was okay. It's not like Daniel was saying he dreaded dinner at home (and so gladly accepted the late meeting as an escape)—no, instead, Daniel was not being forthcoming about how he really felt (he wanted to be home for dinner!). In essence, he was being secretive, and the thing about secrets is that they are a lot of work to keep, and it's helpful to consider if the work of keeping secrets pays off. In Daniel's case, we don't see a strong return on the work of holding that secret. Instead, by saying one thing but wishing the opposite, this type of a secret can breed resentment, regret, and guilt—dark emotions that can compound and flare up.

Notably, Daniel has figured out how to step away from this secretive posture and adopt a new behavior—one of matching what he says with how he feels. "I want to be home for dinner, so no, I can't be at that late meeting." And he candidly reported that this leads to outward disappointment from others who want his time. He noted that this is a consequence he's willing to take.

KEY TAKEAWAY In a world that is now clamoring for flexibility, take great care in how you communicate what flexibility means to you. The thing about flexibility is that it means something different to each person, so craft your own definition and talk about it as well as act on it.

Daniel on the Skill of Conversing

"One of the reasons people feel good talking at work is because the rest of the world has become so uncivil."

Daniel spoke about the environmental cues of the workplace, be it the in-person office or the Zoom cybersphere. Something about this environment, he remarked, cues people to be relatively polite. He pointed out that in the work environment, you may disagree vehemently, but there are still expectations that you do so with a general level of respect and decorum. Why is that true? Daniel went so far as to say that the office is a "safe space," perhaps a counterpoint to the external world where blatant hate-fueled messages and dangerous misinformation are defended as "free speech." In the office, however, Daniel pointed out that there are still some norms for respectful discourse.

KEY TAKEAWAY Embrace the fact that the workplace does differ from the polarized external world; take advantage of the politeness people feel beholden to at work when broaching topics that people need to debate and discuss.

Daniel on the Skill of Listening

> *"My mother always says, 'You have two ears and one mouth,' so you should do twice as much listening as you do talking."*

Like many in the business world, Daniel gets a lot of work done by working a room, talking to people, and making his point known. So, it was interesting to hear his thoughts on how to listen. He described it as a discipline more than as a skill, training himself not to talk so that he can effectively listen. He referenced his mom's adage almost as an accountability technique—if he talks, then he needs to clock in two times the listening time before he talks again. For a savvy businessman like Daniel, we also can assume that he knows how much people like to talk about themselves, so getting someone to verbalize what they are feeling by listening to them well is a valuable trust-building exercise, too.

KEY TAKEAWAY People share valuable information with you when they're talking, so view the time you spend listening as a smart use of time.

Daniel on the Skill of Decision-Making

> *"I have a few trusted people whom I lean on to gauge what's the right thing."*

In his role as a leader, Daniel was clear that it's his job to decide what, when, and how to talk or act on something based on the needs of his community. He was clear that he does not know how to make these decisions alone, and he doesn't just rely on his intuition. Instead, he picks up the phone and calls a tight cohort of his go-to people. He will have a quick chat to understand if a specific news event or controversial topic warrants a conversation, email, 1:1 meeting, etc. He uses this cohort not only to get feedback on what he plans to do but also to find out what others are doing. And, ever the practical mind, he said it is important to use that information to decide if his people really need to hear from him. In some cases, he pointed out, they've already discussed the topic with someone else, and he wouldn't want to be duplicative.

KEY TAKEAWAY Find a couple of people who have their finger on the pulse of what's needed culturally in your organization and build a relationship with them so you can get candid feedback when necessary.

Daniel on the Skill of Representing Others

"I am a fan of the 1:1 conversation. It helps to give voice to those who are afraid to speak up."

As a leader, Daniel thinks he needs facetime with someone in order to represent them effectively. Daniel likes to meet directly with people, as it helps him form a genuine connection, but that can take up his entire day, and his schedule is packed. To manage this, he moves away from the formal, thirty-minute scheduled meetings and instead just calls someone when he has two minutes (yes, two minutes). He rejects the notion that all of these conversations need long, formal discussions. Some do, yes, and his team has convened thoughtful town hall–type discussions, but he finds that his team will also open up in the more casual, impromptu format. To him, it's better that he fit in a two-minute phone call than avoid a topic entirely because he simply doesn't have a thirty-minute slot. And he feels he can cover a lot in those minutes. When asked what kind of discourse he welcomes in the office, Daniel rejected the once-firm notion of certain topics being off-limits. He flat out said that he's learned "nothing is off limits, but there are limitations." He noted that he's not an expert on a lot of the topics that are at the root of today's civic discourse. As he works to learn more, he's been a champion of corporate trainings. Senior leaders may scoff at HR-led trainings, figuring that their time is better spent on billable hours, but not Daniel. He is often the first on his squad to do a training, and, if it's good, he then talks about it incessantly. The content, he said, is often very well done.

KEY TAKEAWAY Don't let "I'm busy" be an excuse for not knowing your people. Fit it in. A lot of short conversations can equip you with a keen understanding of what matters to those whom you represent.

Daniel on the Skill of Persuasion

"Persuasion is rooted in trust, and trust is driven in part by personal integrity. If you want to be a persuasive person, guard your integrity."

Daniel—who loves to immerse himself in data—interestingly cautioned against becoming too reliant on the numbers as a go-to strategy for exerting influence or making a persuasive argument. He noted that a reputation based on performance metrics or other data is fleeting because sometimes factors outside of your control can get in the way and temporarily change your outcomes. In such a case, the statistic you were relying on to make your persuasive point may not be so persuasive after all. Therefore, he noted, you need something else on which to stand—something enduring.

Take this example: Daniel and his team performed incredibly well at work for a six-month stretch. He said, "Our reputational stock couldn't have been higher, and I felt I could use those stats to persuade anyone of anything." However, as he was riding high, a fellow colleague—who was also his informal mentor—warned him to remain humble because performance ebbs and flows and his fortunes would eventually change, not because of his work ethic or ability but simply because that is the cyclical nature of business. Sure enough, his mentor was right. Daniel reflected that whether he is in a season when he is on top of the mountain or in a season when he is in the valley, performance data can be too volatile to rely on as a vehicle for persuasion. Instead, he likes to leverage the part of his reputation that is long-established and unwavering, which is his integrity.

It is his reliably honest nature that is most helpful in moments when he needs to demonstrate power and influence. If you have a reputation for high integrity at work, Daniel would say that is the ultimate currency, even surpassing impressive business statistics—and again, this is from a guy who *loves* an impressive business statistic. In this regard, Daniel might start a challenging conversation around workplace culture—where he's trying to persuade skeptics of a position or action—by anchoring everyone in the social equity that he has built around his high-integrity reputation. Something along the lines of "You know me—I'm reliable, honest, and trustworthy—and I believe [insert idea] is important . . ." Sure, there may be ample data for why that course of action is the right one, but, interestingly, even Daniel might not lead with that.

KEY TAKEAWAY As you are crafting your persuasive strategy at work, consider what established personal attribute may bring the greatest value to the conversation. Is it your integrity, as it is for Daniel, or is it another strong skill that makes people want to say "yes"?

Daniel on the Skill of Forgiveness

> *"We, as a society, do not forgive well. And this gets in the way of our ability to collectively solve problems."*

Daniel's demeanor changed when talking about forgiveness. For someone who prides himself on being able to figure things out quickly, this seemed to stump him. It was as if he were sad that we, as a collective society, are deficient at such an essential skill.

As we continue to unpack the skill of forgiveness, it's helpful to read business professor Rosabeth Moss Kanter's *Harvard Business Review* piece, "Great Leaders Know When to Forgive."[1] She boils the skill of forgiveness down by saying, "instead of settling scores, great leaders make gestures of reconciliation that heal wounds and get on with business." We can then deduce that for a competitive, successful leader such as Daniel, the skill might include:

- *Containing your competitive urge*: Stop thinking about this situation as having winners and losers, as that will ineffectively send you down a path of settling scores.
- *Making a gesture of reconciliation*: Pick up the phone and deliver a genuine apology (we assume that, as someone with strong emotional intelligence and tact, Daniel is quite good at apologies).
- *Getting on with business*: Think of this final point as a relief or reward; for someone as laser focused on business as a Daniel type, it can be a gift to get back to what you do best.

KEY TAKEAWAY Think about the three elements of forgiveness above, consider which of the three is the hardest for you to master, and then focus on it. For example, if Daniel is in fact good at apologies and getting on with business, he can focus on developing the skill of containing his competitive urge.

• • •

In complement to Daniel, please meet Karine, a leader who has held various corporate strategy roles. Karine's experiences include methodically working her way up from junior roles to leadership positions in which she worked in lockstep with top firm leads.

Karine described herself as "very buttoned up" at work, and while she pointed out that she's quite lively outside of work, in the office she carries the reputation of being very serious, even going so far as to say that there's a perception that she's "no fun." This, she said, is because those were the expectations she thought were in place for those hoping to ascend in corporate America, and, to her credit, she has done exceptionally well climbing the ladder. Karine is focused—she does not appear to multitask—so when you have time with her, you should have a clear plan and run the meeting efficiently to accomplish your goals. And then, once your time is up, she will move on to what's next with a warm but quick goodbye. After all, she's busy and needs to get to the next meeting, where she will once again home in and give complete focus. Karine combines this intensity with a quick laugh, a glimpse into her lighthearted side, which she admitted is quite compartmentalized from her professional persona. That bit of humor and levity is surely present, however, and when you get to know Karine, you see that while she takes her work very seriously, she doesn't take herself too seriously. She is affable, funny, and generous with her out-of-work time—she's actively involved in nonprofit work.

As for Karine's journey regarding managing the new expectations of employees, she immediately pointed to George Floyd's murder as a seminal life and career event; she summarized it as "a catalyst for humanity to consider how to spend our time and what to get involved with," which for her included what she called a "discovery journey" to consider some fundamental questions about personal identity.

In the years since then, Karine has seen that leaders need to develop new skills to manage the evolved expectations of employees today, and her perspective on how she's learning those skills follows.

Karine on the Skill of Conversing

"The organization opens the door for others to follow."

Karine explained that the open conversations and forums that are held at work around sensitive topics have always provided a necessary "safe space" for groups to discuss issues of societal or personal significance, but she noted that, increasingly, you see organizations making a firm-wide statement. She spoke about that trend as if it were an invitation for more open conversation at work if someone wants that. This is the power that senior leaders have; while workplace culture certainly manifests at the local team level, the tone does start at the top. Karine emphasized that leaders must issue those firm-wide statements because silence, as far as she is concerned, is "no longer accepted"—neither by employees nor by clients and customers.

KEY TAKEAWAY Even in a working world that increasingly has matrixed reporting lines and flattened hierarchies, the messages that come from leaders are noticed and can set the tone for normative behaviors at work.

Karine on the Skill of Listening

"Meet people where they are."

When Karine spoke about conversing, she noted that a leadership memo opens the door for more conversation if someone wants that. The key word there is "if"—after all, Karine was clear that while some colleagues at work are looking for more open discussion on contentious topics, others don't expect such. The key is in listening for where each individual is regarding their expectations for workplace culture. For example, Karine noted that it's her responsibility to listen for and then ultimately diagnose what the cultural expectation of "bring your authentic self to work" means for different people in her workplace. For some, she noted, that means they want to dress a certain way or do their hair just so, whereas for others it means broaching formerly taboo conversations that could offend others. The line, she noted, is different across generations and functions and is based on personal beliefs. So, that requires her and other managers to carefully listen for what these cultural expectations look like for the various people on their teams.

KEY TAKEAWAY People give information when they are talking (or not talking), and it's a manager's responsibility to use their listening skills to stitch together what that information means about a person's unique perspective on workplace-culture expectations— culture is not a situation where one size fits all.

Karine on the Skill of Representing Others

"I am becoming more comfortable representing others even if their position doesn't directly align with my personal thinking."

Karine noted that her responsibilities as a leader are not always about amplifying what she believes; sometimes they are about using her position of influence to bolster what others believe. She explained that, to do this well, she relies on the compartmental-ization skills that she's developed from having an at-work persona and an out-of-work persona. She's skilled at focusing on a task at hand, and, while working on that with her customary intensity, she can represent the positions of those around her. She was clear to note that empathy is key to doing this well; she can put herself in someone else's shoes and understand why their position is urgent. That empathy leads to an impulse to advocate. And, she pointed out, advocating for one position doesn't mean that she must squash her own point of view. About that balance, she noted: "I can share my view with people and still be in support of other perspectives."

KEY TAKEAWAY In an era when we vilify those with nuanced perspective as "flip-floppers," it's important to point out that peo-ple can consider multiple viewpoints as valid. There is not a lim-ited number of positions for which someone can advocate.

Karine on the Skill of Persuasion

"If I can understand what makes the other person 'tick' or try to identify what they would see in the proposition that benefits them, it makes it easier for me."

Karine views persuasion more as an investigatory pursuit; she has to properly discover what the person she wants to persuade would consider a "win" and then make that possible. So, for her, it's less about winning and more about teeing up her partner to win. For that, she applies several of the former skills of listening and conversing—after all, how better to get someone to tell you what's important than getting them talking? It's an interesting way of considering something like persuasion—or influence—which can have an aggressive association, because in Karine's case, she takes a much more seemingly passive posture. Once she knows her conversational partner's motivations, frustrations, wants, and needs, she can work with that to influence and get her agenda accomplished.

KEY TAKEAWAY Patience can be core to persuasion and influence. Consider how the act of persuasion may not be a bullfight but rather a careful, meticulous process.

Karine on the Skill of Forgiving Others

"I didn't forget, but I got myself to a point where I could focus again."

Karine was recently personally offended at work, and something wasn't handled well, leaving her in a reflective and emotionally bruised state. Tactically speaking, she took time to think—deeply—about what happened and how it made her feel. As the adage goes, time is a powerful salve, and Karine was able to get to a resolution. Notably, the resolution was not with the person or persons who offended her but rather with herself. Her ever-systematic thinking went as follows:

Was I offended? Yes.
Am I a high-integrity person? Yes.
Am I rooted in my personal values? Yes.
But do I want to create a fight? No.

Is this the one thing that would cause me to leave an organization? No.

Do I have the personal resolve to move on? Yes.

For Karine, she was clear that she wasn't forgetting the incident or even really forgiving the offending party. Instead, it appears that she was, in a way, forgiving herself for letting this one slide by because that would position her to return to her work—something that brings her great personal and professional benefit.

KEY TAKEAWAY It takes enormous energy to be mad at someone or something. Sometimes, it can be personally advantageous to summon the will to move on.

• • •

Over the past two chapters, you've met Pastor James, Luisa, Daniel, and Karine. Perhaps your work or life is similar or different from each of them, but in their profiles—and the stories that they shared—it was our intention to equip you with memorable quotes, tangible advice, and "notes from the field" that can be leveraged as we all start, continue, and, hopefully, eventually master the work of adopting these seven skills for managing the evolved expectations of employees today.

15

Notable Counterpoints to Consider

U p to this point, we've covered why leaders and managers need to bolster their business education to manage the evolved expectations of today's employees by adopting a new set of seven skills. Throughout our research, we spoke with many leaders who enthusiastically agreed with this point of view; they confirmed that these skills are the precise ones that managers need to master in order to create a workplace culture that advances the business strategy. However, throughout our research, we also heard from a few leaders who raised important considerations, modifications, or enhancements to this thesis. Issues of people management and workplace culture are rarely black and white, and we wanted to introduce these counterpoints because they illuminate important concerns that today's companies may very well want to consider—or be prepared to manage—as they craft the long-term plan to create a workplace culture that meets the needs of today's employees and bolsters business results.

We like introducing challenges to our thesis because, as we candidly spoke to at the start of the book, we are just two of many, many employees working today and trying to figure out this work, and doing this work well requires a healthy debate on what tactics will work best in the field. So, we've structured this chapter to have the rhythm of a healthy debate. We introduce a counterpoint to our thesis (none of these are a direct hit, but rather nuanced challenges), and then we provide a counterpoint to the counterpoint before summarizing a key takeaway. Consider the following perspectives.

An HR Officer on How the Fear of a Lawsuit Can Hamper Culture Plans

Cam is a seasoned HR professional. Her experience has also straddled multiple geographies, and she speaks with confidence on the nuances of employee expectations across the globe. Cam shared that a legacy fear—she said it dominated corporate HR teams a few decades ago—can drag down culture work. She noted:

> *"[Many people think] you don't want to be offensive because it will be expensive."*

So, counterpoint one is that there are a lot of people who think doing this work is too risky because someone may be offended and take legal action, and thus it's best to avoid it so that you don't incur high legal costs due to litigation. It's important to clarify that when it comes to workplace culture, Cam doesn't live by the objective to avoid a lawsuit, but she said it's a mindset that she's had to work hard to manage with the leaders with whom she works. So, as we discuss this counterpoint further, it's really from the perspective of various people with whom Cam has worked, not Cam herself. Anyway, back to the discussion . . .

Cam described that she's seen several ways to manage a team's fear of a lawsuit, and the tactics have changed decade to decade:

- In the 1980s, there were a lot of trainings, classes, guidelines, and policies about what you could and couldn't say.
- In the 1990s and early 2000s, a better understanding emerged that these trainings, classes, guidelines, etc., should not be created just to avoid discrimination lawsuits, but rather that this work should focus on understanding diversity.
- And now, there has been a trend toward leadership development, specifically on how to see people as an organization's competitive advantage.

And while this evolution is an interesting one—it seems to underscore that even as many workplaces clamor for a "flatter hierarchy," with less responsibility clustered at the top and more of it dispersed to people at all levels—culture work is still largely influenced by leaders (hence the widespread focus on leadership development), or, as Cam would say, culture work is "leader modeled." Cam noted that policies that are handed to all employees can run counter to how humans actually act. People, she summarized, don't always learn by what's written in a manual; instead they may truly learn by watching and practicing, and watching again.

For that, she believes this trend toward leader-modeled behavior change is the right one. She thinks guidebooks that tell employees to respect people can be unproductive in mitigating the risk of a lawsuit, and that instead, the real work is in coaching leaders to act with grace, diplomacy, and smart dialogue skills. Having leaders act in a way that decreases risk—and is good for workplace culture—provides a visible model for what's expected of everyone, and that is the way to avoid a lawsuit.

A Counterpoint to the Counterpoint

If you, like Cam, are having to manage colleagues who believe conversations of political and social significance may be too risky—and expensive—for the workplace, we recommend considering the cost of *not* doing this work. As we noted in chapter two, silence is no longer always perceived as neutral; silence can speak volumes. Our counterpoint, therefore, is that this type of work is no longer avoidable in many work environments. However, that does not mean that teams should adopt an "anything goes" posture at work. Instead, that's precisely why we advocate in this book that people need to be trained to do this work well. Opening the floodgates to these types of conversations at work is certainly risky, but mitigating that risk with focused skill development on the types of ways to navigate such potentially controversial discourse is a risk-mitigation strategy in and of itself. So, we conclude by agreeing with Cam that leadership development is a particularly wise investment for mitigating risk and managing those who challenge that this work may be too expensive to the company from a legal posture.

KEY TAKEAWAY: Risk mitigation at work will always be part of a Chief Human Resource Officer's considerations, and while stated behaviors are increasingly routine in culture frameworks across companies, behavioral policies may be off-putting to some because that's not how people truly learn. There may be an opportunity to frame the role of leaders in modeling good behavior as the evolution of the manuals and trainings that defined workplace culture in previous decades, noting that in today's society, we increasingly learn by watching others instead of scrutinizing and attempting to adhere to policies.

A Finance Professional on Keeping These Conversations Outside of Work

Joe is mid-career and manages a successful team. About that work, he noted:

> *"We rarely talk about [these issues] at work because there's no time at work. People are apprehensive to talk, and we point to lack of time, which perhaps is as an excuse."*

So, counterpoint number two is that there's no time for this at work. Now, Joe went on to immediately catch himself and acknowledge that time pressures are perhaps a convenient excuse (after all, he did explain that he recently took time to go to a sporting event during work hours), but he also noted that his team isn't requesting time to talk about health and societal issues as part of their employee experience. He doesn't think that he is intentionally suppressing an impulse to share opinions; rather, the office remains a place where you don't need to have these discussions. He believes his team would prefer to keep those conversations within the one third of our life that we spend outside of work—he feels that's when you have time to debate and digest the most important issues of our time.

Interestingly, he said the company where he works does send company-wide memos on select issues in the news. And that's where Joe draws an interesting line; he views the company as having the choice to take a stand because that's "the company's position"; however, within his team, he does not follow up with small-group or 1:1 conversations about said issues. And he views that as a sign of respect. He noted that he's not trained to do so, and he thinks his people would prefer to stay focused on work.

A Counterpoint to the Counterpoint

We're certainly not going to counter this point by saying that this work doesn't take time; it most certainly does. But we would say that time spent on managing culture is a smart company investment. The data show that 61 percent of people choose to leave, avoid, or consider employers based on their values and beliefs.[1] That signals that recruiting and retention costs are impacted if you don't take the time to build and maintain a values-driven culture. And what do people want in a values-driven culture? Again, to repeat some data, more people are aware of and care about societal issues than in previous years, with 59 percent of Americans saying it is no longer acceptable for companies to remain silent on social-justice matters and 49 percent saying they assume a company doesn't care about social issues if leaders don't speak out on them (versus only 51 percent demanding strong social and environmental commitments just five years ago).[2] Therefore, we would advocate that Joe and others who share his concerns reposition their thinking from "This culture work takes time away from my work" to "This culture work is part of my work."

KEY TAKEAWAY The workday is very busy, we understand, and managing workplace culture is not easy. There will be many reasons not to do this work (time and emotional exhaustion are just two), but the data signal that this is a wise use of our precious time at work. And if you're on the fence, ask your team. Take this example: a manager may be apprehensive to broach topics of mental health and social issues with the team because they think it will be uncomfortable for the teammates. It's as if a manager might view keeping conversation to work topics as a "gift" to the team. This may be true for some teams, but consider how a leader could confirm that hypothesis with the team. Send an anonymous survey to the group (a question or two in a quick Google Forms survey) and ask if they want to talk about an issue. By asking their team about their preferences, a manager is acting with certainty instead of relying on assumptions.

An Executive on the Role of Operational Change in Workplace Culture

Melissa's expertise as a leader comes through immediately—she homes in on the exact issue at play in seconds and asks precise follow-up questions in a manner that is both wonderfully warm and entirely efficient. Her professional responsibilities are vast, and about managing the evolved expectations of employees and workplace culture, she noted:

> *"We do right by our employees [at the operational*
> *level], but we've pulled back on communications."*

So counterpoint three, our final one, is that the new expectations of employees can be effectively managed by investing in operational changes related to contemporary issues that matter to employees *and* by taking a more selective posture regarding communications. Employee communications on topics related to issues of societal significance can elicit backlash, and we can consider a hypothetical example where employee A might expect a company to take a very different public position on an issue than employee B would—and both of these employees are important to the company.

So what can a leader do? Melissa spoke about operational change as one effective way to demonstrate company values; she gave the example of an employee benefit that has been well received. When asked how employees find out about this benefit without an email or announcement, Melissa pointed to an important communications nuance. "We have benefit changes all the time, and we don't send out firm-wide memos," she said—so, in this case, the company was consistent. However, when an employee asks what the company is doing, that person is then informed of the employee benefit.

Melissa noted that this approach of "doing right by our employees" through operational change is working well, and there has simultaneously been a decrease in critical responses to company communications—after all, there are far fewer communications being sent but no less of an intense focus on supporting employees and living the company's mission, vision, and values.

A Counterpoint to the Counterpoint

Our counterpoint in this case is actually not a counterpoint but a compliment. We agree that operational change is essential. Many companies take an approach opposite of Melissa's and talk, talk, talk—sending out communications on every which topic—but then clam up when it's time to take action. We applaud Melissa's smart strategy to look at the changes that will effect change in the organization, all to bolster a strong culture and retain employees. As for her strategy on reducing the number of communications, we would just add one consideration: sometimes not saying something can be perceived as saying something. Therefore, in cases where not communicating won't work and a company wants or needs to communicate on an issue, consider adding one sentence at the end of a communication that reads something to the effect of "I understand that others may disagree with me." We saw a CEO do this and found it to be a particularly smart strategy.

KEY TAKEAWAY Many have heralded words *and* action as what's needed for business to play an active role in societal progress, perhaps in response to the years—or generations, really—where there have been far too many words but far too little action. Melissa offers a perspective on leading with actions. This may work well for organizations, as it delivers concrete proof points of the types of words that companies put in their values (e.g., "empower our people," "serve the communities where we live and work," "power progress")—all those things need *actions*, just as Melissa emphasized.

• • •

This concludes part four of the book, "Learning from Leaders in Action," where we felt it was important to introduce you to a bevy of working professionals, all reflecting on the concepts in the book. Just as the Chicago Architecture Center—that we mentioned in the introduction—actively encourages its boat tour guides to speak from their own professional experience, we, too, wanted to offer several diverse perspectives as to how to live the principles of this book. It seems you can never attend too many Chicago Architecture Center boat tours, since each one is so remarkably different from the last, and likewise, we could add thousands more "real talk" quotes to this section. We encourage you to now continue this work in the real world. Practice adopting new leadership capabilities, tweak your management style to meet the needs of today's employees, and, most of all, start to develop your own story—your own boat tour, so to speak—about how you learn and live the new skills needed to manage the evolving purpose of workplace culture.

Epilogue: The Power of Partnership

As we've detailed in the previous fifteen chapters, the new purpose of workplace culture requires new skills, skills that many of us weren't taught as part of our education and work experience to date. That's why we've advocated that all managers need to become savvy at seven skills—conversing, listening, empathizing, deciding, representing others, persuading, and forgiving—detailed examples of people who do them well, and discussed the nuts and bolts of how you can learn to master them, too.

But we know that *wanting* to do something and actually *doing* something are two different things. So we close this book with a final recommendation: find a partner with whom you can navigate the new expectations of today's workplace, together. And we don't mean having some people whom you talk to about your management challenges—although that kind of professional support group is also an excellent idea. We advocate that you have a go-to person, a true partner. This partner should be someone with whom you can talk openly about the progress and mistakes you're making, and also someone who can co-facilitate tense conversations, reliably offer candid feedback, push you to try a new policy or procedure, or implore you to consider not implementing a policy or procedure. In essence, someone who views this work as "our" responsibility versus "your" responsibility. Why? Because hard things sometimes feel a little more possible if you're doing them with a partner.

The podcast *Partners* dives into the power of doing something together. Examining professional partnerships across industries, the episodes feature what is possible when you work in lockstep with someone—oftentimes, accomplishing something that you could come up with a million reasons not to do . . . until you found your partner. In one episode about the professional relationship between chef and cookbook author Samin Nosrat and illustrator Wendy MacNaughton, Nosrat shares the origin story of her now best-selling cookbook, *Salt, Fat, Acid, Heat*:

> I didn't actually really want to write this book. I was teaching cooking classes. One of the things I would always talk about is once you understand how salt, fat, acid, and heat work, that's at the basis of all good cooking. And Michael Pollan, who's my writing mentor . . . every week I would bring him a different book idea, and he would always be, "That's bad, that's bad, that's bad." And, eventually, he was, "You have this perfectly good idea, why are you not working on Salt, Fat, Acid, Heat?" And I was, "Because that book won't have beautiful photos."[1]

"Because that book won't have beautiful photos"—that was Nosrat's reason why she wasn't going to wade into a project that was based on such a strong idea. But, as the podcast goes on to share, she wrote the book because she found the right partner in Wendy, whose illustrations are as core to the book as the recipes.

This is similar to our story, too. In our partnership, Elena would certainly convince herself not to write a book because the photos won't be beautiful. Elena is formal and oftentimes apprehensive—reticent to take on something until she determines we are sure that our plan will work. Felicia, however, pushes us to consider try-ing something, confident that if there's a will, then there is a way. But, once we get going, Elena dives into organization, translating a thorny project into an organized, focused plan and working with relentless focus. And Felicia then swoops in, always asking, "What if we . . ."—in essence, pushing and pushing the work product to be sure it is positively stellar. This is our working partnership, and because we have each other, we take on things that scare us—things like managing the new purpose of workplace culture.

While we advocate that all managers should acknowledge and learn the skills we discussed in this book, we are realistic that this is asking a lot of you. It's asking you to wade into some-thing nuanced, time consuming, and with a high likelihood of stumbling—on top of continuing the work in your job description. Today's workplace expectations are also evolving and will have constant new nuances to consider. That's why we should all have our partners by our side for this work. Not so that you can split the work—but rather so that you can do the work a bit better than if you were to approach it as a solo venture. Consider that, in some situations, your partner will flag a reason to do something when you are laser focused on all the reasons not to do it. In other situa-tions, your partner will implore you not to do something when your impulse is to take immediate action. We know this because it's the precise dynamic that we have in our professional work, our teaching, and our writing. The contrasting skills that we bring to each other allow us to do our best work, together. And perhaps just as important, our partnership makes sure work isn't lonely. Working to manage the new purpose of workplace culture should not be a lonely venture, full stop. Find a partner.

Acknowledgments

We heard a CEO say something a few years ago that left us both emphatically nodding: "I've never seen anyone become the best in their field who didn't outwork everyone else." We turned to each other upon hearing that, both smiling, and said, "Yes!"

Working hard(er) has been our approach to navigating the professional world, and while writing this book, we certainly tapped into that strategy. We worked harder than ever. However, we have come to realize that it doesn't just take hard work; you also need to have confidence that the hard work will pay off. Our confidence comes in part from having an amazing community of support. This community is comprised of hundreds of incredible, driven, and generous people, but six stand out to us because they regularly say—without hesitation—that they believe in us. That is a sacred gift that we don't take for granted because when they speak about their belief in us, we are reminded to believe in ourselves and to strive forward with confidence, and that confidence fuels us to persist.

We would like to acknowledge:

Josh Grotto, Elena's husband. As an artist, he models daily how to work through the anxiety of staring at a blank canvas—or, in our case, a blank page. He is proof that when you methodically put in hours and hours of work, you can create something remarkable. Thank you, Josh, for so much.

Sirretha Joy, Felicia's mother, a retired US Army master sergeant who served twenty-seven years in the military. She has always been as tough as nails and demonstrated by example that a person can work their way to the top with focus, grit, and determination—even if they have to occasionally work around a few people who do not welcome them. She applauds us for endeavoring to create workplace cultures where all are respected, included, given the sense that they belong, and provided the opportunity to apply their talents and excel.

Chris Peeler, Felicia's big brother, who was her biggest fan and cheered for her more than the most boisterous sports fans. His untimely passing was the greatest loss she ever felt. During her time of grieving, her colleagues and managers showed the most amazing support. She was surprised and blessed by their care, demonstrating the true power of workplace culture to touch and change people's lives.

Cydney Roach, a visionary thinker who believes that the workplace can be a venue for experiences that change lives. She has been our treasured teacher and mentor at Edelman—helping to spark an interest in the topic of workplace culture by sharing so much of her vast mind. She stirs us with her incredible creativity and verve.

Sheila Mulligan, the fierce and impactful leader at Edelman who was running the Corporate Advisory practice when we both joined the firm. She is a force to be reckoned with and sharpened both of us early on by speaking with belief and certainty about our unique skills and strengths—and by setting the tone for excellence as a critical aspect of our team culture.

Ryan Cudney, our dear colleague and manager at Edelman. An unwavering advocate for us who often talks about how he hires people who are smarter than he is, when in reality we are constantly in awe of his brilliance, work ethic, and genuine kindness. He is one of our greatest inspirations and has helped us become better professionals and better people. We are forever grateful.

Notes

Chapter 1

1. Dean Mobbs et al., "The Ecology of Human Fear: Survival Optimization and the Nervous System," *Frontiers in Neuroscience* 9 (March 2015): 55, doi:10.3389/fnins.2015.00055.

2. "'Nothing else in the world . . . not all the armies . . . is so powerful as an idea whose time has come.'–Victor Hugo, The Future of Man. From the series Great Ideas of Western Man," Smithsonian American Art Museum, accessed June 22, 2023, https://americanart.si.edu/artwork/nothing-else -worldnot-all-armiesis-so-powerful-idea-whose-time-has-come-victor-hugo -future.

3. Brian Kropp, "9 Trends That Will Shape Work in 2021 and Beyond," *Harvard Business Review*, January 14, 2021, https://hbr.org/2021/01/9-trends -that-will-shape-work-in-2021-and-beyond?utm_medium=email&utm _source=tgr_regengagement&utm_campaign=signin_regs_v202102&hid eIntromercial=true&deliveryName=DM126156.

4. Ibid.

5. Katherine Schaeffer, "10 Facts About Today's College Graduates," Pew Research Center, April 12, 2022, https://www.pewresearch.org/fact-tank /2022/04/12/10-facts-about-todays-college-graduates/.

6. "What Percentage of Americans Currently Live in the Town or City Where They Grew Up?" North American Van Lines, accessed June 22, 2023, https://www.northamerican.com/infographics/where-they-grew-up.

7. Abby Budiman, "Americans Are More Positive About the Long-Term Rise in U.S. Racial and Ethnic Diversity Than in 2016," Pew Research Center,

October 1, 2020, https://www.pewresearch.org/short-reads/2020/10/01
/americans-are-more-positive-about-the-long-term-rise-in-u-s-racial-and
-ethnic-diversity-than-in-2016/.

8. Benjamin Harris, "Racial Inequality in the United States," US Department
of the Treasury, July 21, 2022, https://home.treasury.gov/news/featured
-stories/racial-inequality-in-the-united-states.

9. Anthony P. Carnevale et al., "Born to Win, Schooled to Lose: Why Equally
Talented Students Don't Get Equal Chances to Be All They Can Be," George-
town University Center on Education and the Workforce, 2019, https://cew
.georgetown.edu/wp-content/uploads/FR-Born_to_win-schooled_to_lose
.pdf.

10. "2021 Porter Novelli Business & Social Justice Study," Porter Novelli,
May 5, 2021, https://www.porternovelli.com/findings/2021-porter-novelli
-business-social-justice-study/.

11. "Generational Differences in the Workplace [Infographic]," Purdue
Global, accessed June 22, 2023, https://www.purdueglobal.edu/education
-partnerships/generational-workforce-differences-infographic/.

12. "The Year Employees Restructure Their Relationship with Work," 2023
Employee Experience Trends Report, Qualtrics, accessed April 17, 2023,
https://www.qualtrics.com/ebooks-guides/2023-ex-trends-report/.

13. Julie Coffman, Bianca Bax, Alex Noether, and Brenen Blair, "The Fabric of
Belonging: How to Weave an Inclusive Culture," Bain & Company, accessed
April 17, 2023, https://www.bain.com/insights/the-fabric-of-belonging-how
-to-weave-an-inclusive-culture/.

14. Jordan Turner, "Employees Seek Personal Value and Purpose at Work.
Be Prepared to Deliver," Gartner, March 29, 2023, https://www.gartner
.com/en/articles/employees-seek-personal-value-and-purpose-at-work-be
-prepared-to-deliver.

15. "Mental Health in the Workplace: The Coming Revolution," McKinsey
Quarterly, McKinsey & Company, December 8, 2020, https://www
.mckinsey.com/industries/healthcare/our-insights/mental-health-in-the
-workplace-the-coming-revolution.

16. "2021 Edelman Trust Barometer," Edelman, accessed June 22, 2023,
https://www.edelman.com/sites/g/files/aatuss191/files/2021-03/2021
%20Edelman%20Trust%20Barometer.pdf.

17. "2019 Edelman Trust Barometer Special Report: Institutional Investors," Edelman, accessed April 17, 2023, https://www.edelman.com/research/2019-edelman-trust-barometer-special-report-institutional-investors.

18. Jack McCullough, "Bill George, Ex-Medtronic CEO, on the Common Traits of Successful Leaders," *Forbes*, December 7, 2022, https://www.forbes.com/sites/jackmccullough/2022/12/07/bill-george-ex-medtronic-ceo-on-the-common-traits-of-successful-leaders/?sh=56c32d6777ca.

19. "2022 Edelman Trust Barometer," Edelman, accessed June 22, 2023, https://www.edelman.com/sites/g/files/aatuss191/files/2022-01/2022%20Edelman%20Trust%20Barometer%20FINAL_Jan25.pdf.

20. Evan W. Carr et al., "The Value of Belonging at Work," *Harvard Business Review*, December 16, 2019, https://hbr.org/2019/12/the-value-of-belonging-at-work.

Chapter 2

1. Michael J. de la Merced, "Eastman Kodak Files for Bankruptcy," *New York Times*, January 19, 2012, https://archive.nytimes.com/dealbook.nytimes.com/2012/01/19/eastman-kodak-files-for-bankruptcy/.

2. James Estrin, "Kodak's First Digital Moment," *New York Times*, August 12, 2015, https://archive.nytimes.com/lens.blogs.nytimes.com/2015/08/12/kodaks-first-digital-moment/.

3. "6.5 Million Firestone Tires Recalled Because of Link to Fatalities," *New York Times*, August 9, 2000, https://www.nytimes.com/2000/08/09/business/65-million-firestone-tires-recalled-because-of-link-to-fatalities.html.

4. "Firestone's Tire Recall," Center for Ethical Organizational Cultures, Auburn University, accessed April 18, 2023, https://harbert.auburn.edu/binaries/documents/center-for-ethical-organizational-cultures/cases/firestone.pdf.

5. Alan B. Krueger and Alexandre Mas, "Strikes, Scabs and Tread Separations: Labor Strife and the Production of Defective Bridgestone/Firestone Tires," National Bureau of Economic Research Working Paper Series, February 2003, https://www.nber.org/system/files/working_papers/w9524/w9524.pdf.

6. "Enhancing Job Satisfaction, Pride," Bridgestone, accessed April 18, 2023, https://www.bridgestone.com/responsibilities/social/human_rights/labor_practices/index.html; "Human Rights, Labor Practices," Bridgestone, accessed April 18, 2023, https://www.bridgestone.com/responsibilities/social/human_rights/.

7. "Founding," Delta Flight Museum, accessed April 18, 2023, https://www.deltamuseum.org/exhibits/delta-history/founding.

8. Holly Brubach, "You Don't Need More Willpower," *O, The Oprah Magazine*, January 2009, https://www.oprah.com/spirit/professors-kegan-and-lahey-on-the-challenges-of-change/all.

Chapter 3

1. Randall Beck and Jim Harter, "Managers Account for 70% of Variance in Employee Engagement," Gallup, April 21, 2015, https://news.gallup.com/businessjournal/182792/managers-account-variance-employee-engagement.aspx.

2. 2022 Edelman Trust Barometer Special Report: Trust in the Workplace, accessed April 18, 2023, https://www.edelman.com/sites/g/files/aatuss191/files/2022-08/2022%20Edelman%20Trust%20Barometer%20Special%20Report%20Trust%20in%20the%20Workplace%20FINAL.pdf.

3. "Transform with Mental Fitness: How Organizations Reach Their Peak," BetterUp, July 14, 2022, YouTube video, 1:02, https://youtu.be/CL_hFzK5-vQ.

4. "Dear CEO: Here's Why You Should Trust Your Employees," Edelman, accessed April 18, 2023, https://www.edelman.com/trust/2022-trust-barometer/special-report-trust-workplace/dear-ceo-heres-why-you-should-trust-your-employees.

5. Megan Cole, "What Makes a Good Manager: The Case for Listening and Assessing Skills," ATD, March 21, 2016, https://www.td.org/insights/what-makes-a-good-manager-the-case-for-listening-and-assessing-skills.

6. Brooke Deterline, "The Power of Forgiveness at Work," *Greater Good* magazine, August 26, 2016, https://greatergood.berkeley.edu/article/item/the_power_of_forgiveness_at_work.

7. "Ideas Worth Teaching," Aspen Institute, accessed April 18, 2023, https://www.ideasworthteachingawards.com/about.

8. "HBS' Institute for the Study of Business in Global Society Names Inaugural Cohort of Visiting Fellows," *Harvard Gazette*, April 21, 2022, https://news.harvard.edu/gazette/story/newsplus/hbs-institute-for-the-study-of-business-in-global-society-names-inaugural-cohort-of-visiting-fellows/.

Chapter 4

1. Rebecca Newton, "HR Can't Change Company Culture by Itself," *Harvard Business Review*, November 2, 2016, https://hbr.org/2016/11/hr-cant-change-company-culture-by-itself.
2. Denise Lee Yohn, "Company Culture Is Everyone's Responsibility," *Harvard Business Review*, February 8, 2021, https://hbr.org/2021/02/company-culture-is-everyones-responsibility.

Chapter 5

1. "The Evolution of Diversity," NSCIVICBLOG, Penn State University, January 27, 2016, https://sites.psu.edu/nscivicblog/2016/01/27/the-evolution-of-diversity/.
2. "About Us," Business Roundtable (website), accessed April 20, 2023, https://www.businessroundtable.org/about-us.
3. Duke Today Staff, "Americans Have Fewer Friends Outside the Family, Duke Study Shows," *Duke Today*, June 23, 2006, https://today.duke.edu/2006/06/socialisolation.html.
4. "New Surgeon General Advisory Raises Alarm About the Devastating Impact of the Epidemic of Loneliness and Isolation in the United States," US Department of Health and Human Services, May 3, 2023, https://www.hhs.gov/about/news/2023/05/03/new-surgeon-general-advisory-raises-alarm-about-devastating-impact-epidemic-loneliness-isolation-united-states.html.

Chapter 6

1. Lou Solomon, "The Top Complaints from Employees About Their Leaders," *Harvard Business Review*, June 24, 2015, https://hbr.org/2015/06/the-top-complaints-from-employees-about-their-leaders.

2. Michael Yeomans et al., "Conversational Receptiveness: Improving Engagement with Opposing Views," *Organizational Behavior and Human Decision Processes* 160 (September 2020): 131–48, doi:10.1016/j.obhdp .2020.03.011.

3. Nathan M. Fulham, Kori L. Krueger, Taya R. Cohen, "Honest Feedback: Barriers to Receptivity and Discerning the Truth in Feedback," *Current Opinion in Psychology* 46 (August 2022): 101405, doi:10.1016/j.copsyc .2022.101405.

4. "Manager Conversations," The Ohio State University Office of Human Resources, accessed April 24, 2023, https://gatewaytolearning.osu.edu /leadership-development/manager-conversations/.

5. "Celeste Headlee: 10 Ways to Have a Better Conversation | TED," TED, March 8, 2016, YouTube video, 11:44, https://youtu.be/R1vskiVDwl4.

6. "The Trust 10," Edelman Trust Barometer 2022, accessed April 24, 2023, https://www.edelman.com/sites/g/files/aatuss191/files/2022-09/Trust %2022_Top10_workplace.pdf.

Chapter 7

1. Rebecca D. Minehart, Benjamin B. Symon, and Laura K. Rock, "What's Your Listening Style?," *Harvard Business Review*, May 31, 2022, https://hbr .org/2022/05/whats-your-listening-style.

2. Seth S. Horowitz, "The Science and Art of Listening," *New York Times*, November 9, 2012, https://www.nytimes.com/2012/11/11/opinion/sunday /why-listening-is-so-much-more-than-hearing.html.

3. Bernard T. Ferrari, "The Executive's Guide to Better Listening," *McKinsey Quarterly*, February 1, 2012, https://www.mckinsey.com/featured-insights /leadership/the-executives-guide-to-better-listening.

Chapter 8

1. Andrew Alexander King (@andrew_alexander_king), Instagram post, October 28, 2022, https://www.instagram.com/p/CkP_zQFtcvW/?hl=en.

2. Jamil Zaki, "Leading with Empathy in Turbulent Times: A Practical Guide," Edelman, 2021.

3. "Insights from the Marine Corps Organizational Culture Research Project: Empathy in Leadership," Center for Advanced Operational Culture Learning, June 1, 2020, https://www.usmcu.edu/Portals/218/MCOCR%20QL%20Empathy_in_Leadership%20060120.pdf.

4. Ibid.

5. Zaki, "Leading with Empathy in Turbulent Times."

6. Susan Peppercorn, "5 Questions Every Manager Needs to Ask Their Direct Reports," *Harvard Business Review,* January 21, 2022, https://hbr.org/2022/01/5-questions-every-manager-needs-to-ask-their-direct-reports.

7. Solomon, "The Top Complaints from Employees About Their Leaders."

Chapter 9

1. "Is Trust the Ultimate Currency of Stakeholder Capitalism?," The Aspen Institute, June 27, 2022, YouTube video, 46:12, https://www.youtube.com/watch?v=qj9CItmedPk&t=935s.

Chapter 11

1. Adam Ferree, "The Difference Between Negotiation and Persuasion," LinkedIn, May 3, 2021, https://www.linkedin.com/pulse/difference-between-negotiation-persuasion-adam-ferree/.

2. Scott Galloway, "Principles of Persuasion—with Bob Cialdini," May 6, 2021, in *The Prof G Pod with Scott Galloway,* Vox Media Podcast Network, podcast.

3. Robert Cialdini, *Influence, New and Expanded: The Psychology of Persuasion* (New York: Harper Business, 2021).

Chapter 12

1. "What Is Forgiveness?," *Greater Good* magazine, accessed April 25, 2023, https://greatergood.berkeley.edu/topic/forgiveness/definition.

2. Brooke Deterline, "The Power of Forgiveness at Work," *Greater Good* magazine, August 26, 2016, https://greatergood.berkeley.edu/article/item/the_power_of_forgiveness_at_work.

3. Loren Toussaint et al., "Forgiveness Working: Forgiveness, Health and Productivity in the Workplace," *American Journal of Health Promotion* 32, no. 1 (August 2016), doi:10.1177/0890117116662312; "REACH Forgiveness of Others," Everett Worthington (website), accessed April 26, 2023, http://www.evworthington-forgiveness.com/reach-forgiveness-of-others.

Chapter 13

1. John F. Magee, "Decision Trees for Decision-Making," *Harvard Business Review*, July 1964, https://hbsp.harvard.edu/product/64410-PDF-ENG.

Chapter 14

1. Rosabeth Moss Kanter, "Great Leaders Know When to Forgive," *Harvard Business Review*, February 26, 2013, https://hbr.org/2013/02/great-leaders-know-when-to.

Chapter 15

1. Richard Edelman, "The Belief-Driven Employee," Edelman, August 31, 2021, https://www.edelman.com/trust/2021-trust-barometer/belief-driven-employee/new-employee-employer-compact.
2. 2021 Porter Novelli Business & Social Justice Study.

Epilogue

1. Samin Nosrat, "Samin Nosrat & Wendy MacNaughton," February 5, 2020, in *Partners*, Hrishikesh Hirway and Mailchimp, podcast, https://partners.show/.

Index

About the Authors

Credit: Maria Ponce Photography

Elena Grotto (right) holds a leadership position in business transformation consulting, where she advises senior decision-makers at Fortune 500 companies as they stabilize the workforce during a period of significant change. In complement to her corporate work, Elena teaches, writes, and speaks regularly on emerging issues pertaining to business transformation and the evolved expectations of today's workforce. This includes her role on the faculty at the University of Chicago Booth School of Business, from where she holds an MBA degree.

Felicia Joy (left) is a leading executive on business strategy, organizational transformation, and behavior change. She counsels and works alongside leaders in many industries, including aviation, manufacturing, healthcare, energy, biopharma, and financial services, to navigate and solve thorny business problems that have disrupted their people and profits. Additionally, Felicia uses her unique skill set and experiences to write, speak, and teach on culture, measurement, and strategic business performance. She is a faculty member at the University of Chicago Booth School of Business and earned her master's degree in behavioral science at Harvard.

Learn more about the authors at joygrotto.com.